Euripides: *Children of Heracles*

COMPANIONS TO GREEK AND ROMAN TRAGEDY

Series Editor: Thomas Harrison

Aeschylus: Agamemnon, Barbara Goward
Aeschylus: Eumenides, Robin Mitchell-Boyask
Aeschylus: Libation Bearers, C. W. Marshall
Aeschylus: Persians, David Rosenbloom
Aeschylus: Prometheus Bound, I. A. Ruffell
Aeschylus: Seven Against Thebes, Isabelle Torrance
Aeschylus: Suppliants, Thalia Papadopoulou
Euripides: Alcestis, Niall W. Slater
Euripides: Bacchae, Sophie Mills
Euripides: Cyclops, Carl A. Shaw
Euripides: Hecuba, Helene P. Foley
Euripides: Heracles, Emma Griffiths
Euripides: Hippolytus, Sophie Mills
Euripides: Ion, Laura Swift
Euripides: Iphigenia at Aulis, Pantelis Michelakis
Euripides: Medea, William Allan
Euripides: Orestes, Matthew Wright
Euripides: Phoenician Women, Thalia Papadopoulou
Euripides: Suppliant Women, Ian Storey
Euripides: Trojan Women, Barbara Goff
Seneca: Hercules Furens, Neil W. Bernstein
Seneca: Medea, Helen Slaney
Seneca: Oedipus, Susanna Braund
Seneca: Phaedra, Roland Mayer
Seneca: Thyestes, Peter Davis
Sophocles: Antigone, Douglas Cairns
Sophocles: Ajax, Jon Hesk
Sophocles: Electra, Michael Lloyd
Sophocles: Oedipus at Colonus, Adrian Kelly
Sophocles: Philoctetes, Hanna Roisman
Sophocles: Women of Trachis, Brad Levett

Euripides: *Children of Heracles*

Florence Yoon

BLOOMSBURY ACADEMIC
LONDON • NEW YORK • OXFORD • NEW DELHI • SYDNEY

BLOOMSBURY ACADEMIC
Bloomsbury Publishing Plc
50 Bedford Square, London, WC1B 3DP, UK
1385 Broadway, New York, NY 10018, USA
29 Earlsfort Terrace, Dublin 2, Ireland

BLOOMSBURY, BLOOMSBURY ACADEMIC and the Diana logo
are trademarks of Bloomsbury Publishing Plc

First published in Great Britain 2020
Paperback edition first published 2021

Cover design: Terry Woodley
Cover image © Karneia Painter's Herakles and Alkmene pelike.
Museo Nazionale della Siritide, Policoro.

A catalogue record for this book is available from the British Library.

Library of Congress Cataloging-in-Publication Data
Names: Yoon, Florence, 1981-author.
Title: Euripides, Children of Heracles / Florence Yoon.
Other titles: Companions to Greek and Roman tragedy.
Description: New York: Bloomsbury Academic, 2020. |
Series: Companions to Greek and Roman tragedy |
Includes bibliographical references and index. |
Summary: "This book is an accessible guide through the many twists and turns of Euripides'
Children of Heracles, providing several frameworks through which to understand and
appreciate the play. Children of Heracles follows the fortunes of Heracles' family after his death.
Euripides confronts characters and audience alike with an extraordinary series of plot twists
and ethical challenges as the persecuted family of refugees struggles to find asylum in
Athens before taking revenge on its enemy Eurystheus. It is a fast-paced story that explores the
nature of power and its abuse, focusing on the appropriate treatment and behaviour of the powerless
and the obligations and limitations of asylum. The audience must continually re-evaluate the play's moral
dimensions as the characters respond to complications that range from the fantastic to the frighteningly
realistic. Yoon situates Children of Heracles in its literary context, showing how Euripides constructs
a unique kind of tragic plot from a wide range of conventions. It also explores the centrality of the dead
Heracles and the leading role given to the socially powerless and the dramatically marginal.
Finally, it discusses the historical contexts of the play's original performance and its political
resonance both then and now"– Provided by publisher.
Identifiers: LCCN 2019039153 (print) | LCCN 2019039154 (ebook) |
ISBN 9781350076754 (hardback) | ISBN 9781350076761 (ebook) | ISBN 9781350076778 (epub)
Subjects: LCSH: Euripides. Children of Heracles.
Classification: LCC PA3978 .Y66 2020 (print) | LCC PA3978 (ebook) | DDC882/.01–dc23
LC record available at https://lccn.loc.gov/2019039153
LC ebook record available at https://lccn.loc.gov/2019039154

ISBN: HB: 978-1-3500-7675-4
PB: 978-1-3501-9387-1
ePDF: 978-1-3500-7676-1
eBook: 978-1-3500-7677-8

Series: Companions to Greek and Roman Tragedy

Typeset by RefineCatch Limited, Bungay, Suffolk

To find out more about our authors and books visit
www.bloomsbury.com and sign up for our newsletters.

Contents

List of Figures   vi

Preface   x

1   Action and Expectation   1

2   Summing the Parts   19

3   Heracles and Other Imagined Figures   43

4   The Power of the Weak   61

5   Then and Now   87

Appendix: Fragments   115

Selected Chronology   117

Guide to Further Reading   119

Notes   123

Bibliography   145

Index   157

Figures

1 Map of significant places viii

2 Outline of the play's action 6

3 Schematic of possible initial positioning, given a performance space roughly 25 metres in diameter 7

4 Outline of plot patterns 35

5 A typical depiction of Eurystheus and Heracles. Attic amphora, mid-sixth *c.* BCE. London, British Museum 56

6 Late fifth-*c.* BCE Lucanian *pelike*, 44.5 cm. Policoro, Museo Nazionale della Siritide 98

7 Late fifth-*c.* BCE Lucanian column-*krater*, 52 cm. Berlin, Staatliche Museen 99

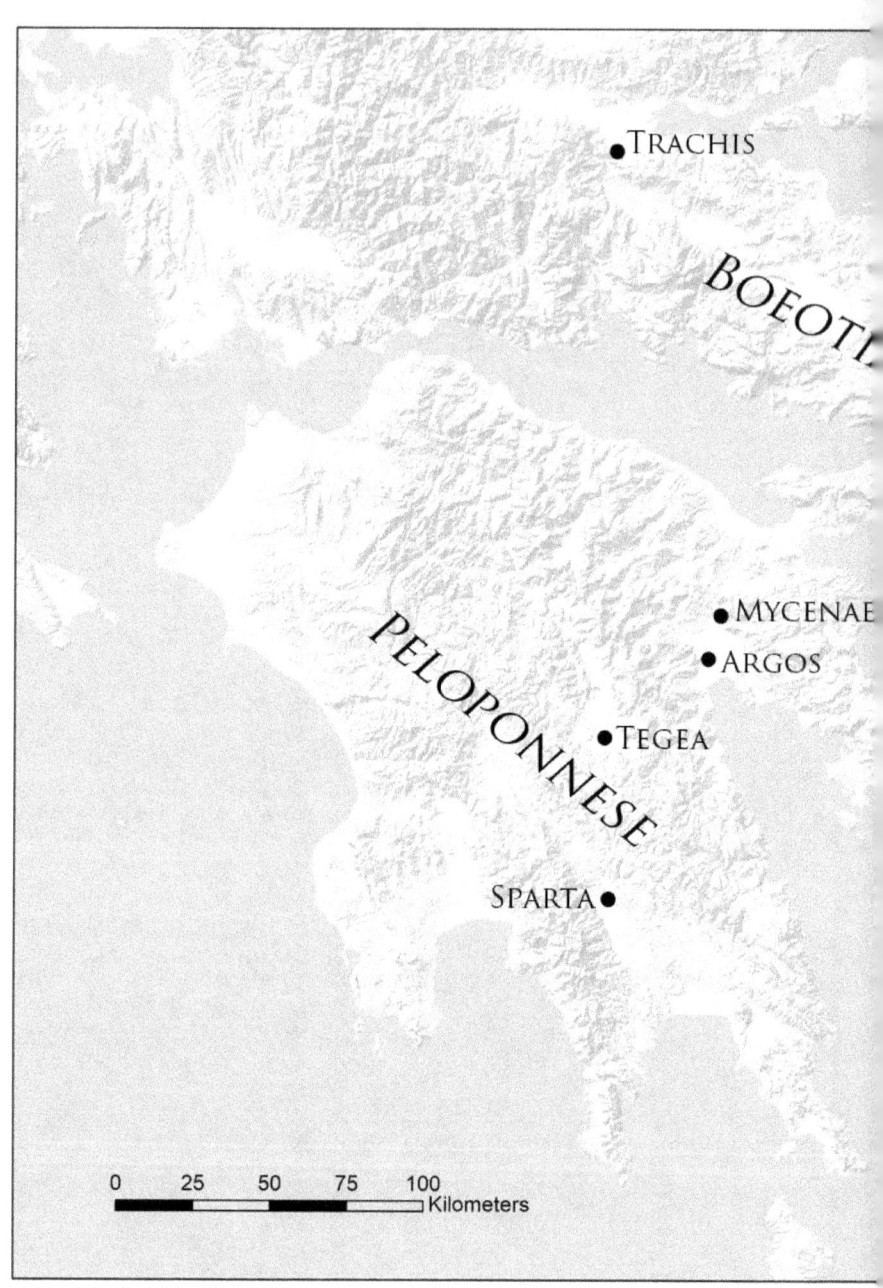

Fig. 1 Map of significant places.

EUBOIA

ATTICA

●MARATHON

●ATHENS

●Thebes

●Plataea

MARATHON●
TETRAPOLIS

Megara ●SKIRONIAN
CLIFFS ●Eleusis

PALLENE

●Athens

0   25   50
                   Kilometers

Sources: Esri, USGS, NOAA

Preface

Children of Heracles, also known by various spellings of its Greek title *Heraclidae,* is a swift-moving and elusive play. This book aims to help readers appreciate the whole as greater than the sum of its parts by suggesting several angles that capture the essential changeability of the play in both its plot and characters. By suggesting alternative frameworks for the same material, I hope to help my readers not only to find one that rings true to them, but also to appreciate the range of audiences that Euripides was composing for. This does result in a certain degree of overlap between chapters, but I hope that the perspective offered by this approach will make up for any drawbacks.

I have written this book making three related assumptions about its readers. First, that you have recently read (or seen) the play, and that you will return to the play afterwards. Second, that this is not the first Greek tragedy you have read or seen, and you have some point of comparison. (Although this play could be an excellent introduction to the genre, I know no one for whom this has been the first port of call.) Third, that you have come to this play with some sense of the historical context of the fifth century BCE, though the details may elude you. For example, you are likely to know that the Peloponnesian War involved Sparta and Athens, though you may not be able to place either city on a map, or to remember any of the dates or the specific battles. In case I have assumed too much or too little I have included refreshers about the most essential details, and have provided references to the Greek and the secondary literature in the notes (though for ease of access I have tried to prioritize English-language scholarship, and articles over monographs). I hope that scholars and students alike will find some fresh ideas here and a starting-point for new investigations.

My thanks to the many friends and colleagues who have shared their support and expertise during the writing of this book. Special thanks to Susanna Braund, who guided me into this project; to Lucy Jackson, who helped me through various struggles; to Sheri Pak and Geoff Wilde, who lent their technical skills; and to Matt McCarty, who read the whole draft and drew me a map while I was working my way out.

All translations are my own.

The book is dedicated to my parents and my children, τοὺς μὲν γέροντας, τοὺς δὲ νηπίους ἔτι (956).

1

Action and Expectation

Children of Heracles is an unusually action-packed, fast-paced play. In recounting the fortunes of Heracles' family after his death, Euripides gives us a pitiful refugee tableau, a sudden and sacrilegious attack, an unexpected rescue, a divine demand for human sacrifice, a willing victim, a pseudo-comic scene, a battle narrative, a miraculous rejuvenation and a vicious triumph – all in just over a thousand lines. With every scene Euripides suggests a new direction for the play, only to turn us around again in the next. In performance the intensity of each scene carries the audience along rather like a modern action film, but those looking for the bigger picture – particularly readers with more leisure to consider the play's artistic merits – can find these twists and turns more challenging. This chapter focuses on the action of the play and the shifting expectations that it creates.

Our reading of the play must rely almost entirely on the evidence provided by the text itself because we have few external clues to guide us. *Children of Heracles* is one of the nine plays often called 'alphabetic' which have survived by chance, as they belonged to what seems to be the only volume – E to K – to be preserved in a single copy from a complete alphabetic collection of Euripides' plays.[1] No information about the play's original performance has been transmitted with it. Accordingly, we do not know exactly when it was produced, but it seems to be one of the earliest extant plays of Euripides, probably dating before 425 BCE and possibly as early as 455 BCE.[2] We can assume that, like all extant tragedies, it was written for outdoor performance at one of two competitive festivals before an audience composed of both Athenian and non-Athenian spectators.[3] If so, it was written and performed with at least one other tragedy (at the Lenaia festival) or with two other tragedies and a satyr-play[4] (at the City Dionysia), but we do not know what those other plays were, or how they might have influenced the audience's experience of our play.

Despite the lack of precise contextual information, we can make some general deductions about the audience's initial state of knowledge. Following this, we will turn to the play itself, laying out as simply as possible the events of each scene, including the controversial ending, and considering the audience's changing state of knowledge and expectations as the play progresses. Included in this outline are important elements of staging, which are essential to our understanding of the play but which we must reconstruct from textual indications as the plays come to us with no indications of stage action or movement.[5]

Audience anticipations

What would the original audience of *Children of Heracles* have known or guessed about the play they were waiting to see?[6] There are three sources we can consider as likely to have shaped the audience's expectations of any Greek tragedy as they sat down for the performance. Our knowledge of each of these sources is extremely limited, and the audience itself would have been made up of very different kinds of people with different access to these sources. Nevertheless, it is useful to keep in mind the kinds of expectations that Euripides had to work with.

The first source for the Greek audience is traditional mythology, from which most tragedies drew their plots.[7] It is impossible to state with any confidence just what a given audience would have known; in addition to the diversity in the audience, the myths themselves are full of variations, many of which have not been preserved. The versions most familiar to us now are often familiar precisely because of a particularly influential tragedy. However, we do know that while Heracles was one of the most famous figures of mythology then as today, ubiquitous in art and literature as well as one of the most widely worshipped cultic heroes, his children did not share his popularity. Their story seems to be a much later development from their father's; we do not have evidence for the mythology of the Heraclids before the fifth century,[8] and our records of their cults in several Attic communities date from the fourth century.[9] It is tempting to try to distinguish which details of our play's plot were traditional and which were Euripidean inventions, but such efforts must remain speculative.

However, we do have evidence that the story of the Heraclids played an important role in how fifth-century cities in Attica and the Peloponnese shaped their identities. This is best demonstrated in an account given by Herodotus, whose *Histories* are approximately contemporary with our play. Herodotus recounts that as the Greeks prepared to engage the Persians at Plataea in 479 BCE, in one of the most important battles of the Persian War, a dispute arose between the Tegeans (inhabitants of a powerful city in the central Peloponnese) and the Athenians over precedence of position (9.26–28.1). Each side supports its claim in part by recounting its role in the Heraclid legend. The Tegeans argue that the more prestigious position is one of the particular privileges granted to them long ago by the other Peloponnesians, because when the Heraclids first tried to return to their ancestral Peloponnesian home after the death of Eurystheus, the Tegean king was the champion who fought and killed Heracles' son Hyllus in single combat, and secured for the Peloponnese a hundred years of protection from Heraclid invasions. Herodotus' Athenians respond to this claim with five stories, the first of which is a brief version of the one that forms the basis of our play: that when the Heraclids were being persecuted by Eurystheus, Athens alone defended them and defeated the invading Peloponnesians. The myths are used here to express political identity; Herodotus' Tegeans present themselves as defenders of the Peloponnese against Heraclid invaders, while his Athenians present themselves as defenders of the Heraclids against Peloponnesian persecution.[10] Herodotus' account cannot be accepted as a record of an actual debate, but it shows both the prevalence and importance of such stories in the time of our play, and these two particular stories – the Athenian defence of the Heraclids and the 'return of the Heraclids' to the Peloponnese several generations later – are crucial background knowledge for our play.

The second possible source of information – if the play was performed at the City Dionysia festival – would have been the *proagōn*, a formal ceremony that took place about a week before the performances themselves. Once again, our information is limited,[11] but we do know that the poet gave a speech to introduce the play, and that a significant part of the audience would have heard it, though the audience of the *proagōn* could not have been as big as the audience of the plays themselves. We may compare the concept (if not the content) of the modern film trailer; the poet is likely to have sketched an outline of the general plot without giving away the details of how it would resolve or any innovations that depended on surprise for their effect. It is possible that the cast of the play had some role in this presentation; we know that the chorus and actors were present, but as they did not wear their masks and costumes it is unlikely that scenes of any length were performed. The playwright would have had almost complete control over how much information to give the audience, and this will have played an important part in shaping audience expectations.

The third source available to some members of the Greek audience would have been other plays written along similar lines. We will return to this possibility later, but it is worth noting here that we know of another play called *Children of Heracles* written and produced by Aeschylus, which must have preceded our play. Only four brief fragments of the play survive, none of which gives any indication of the shape of the plot as a whole. Titles of plays can be misleading[12] – Aeschylus and Euripides both wrote plays called *Suppliant Women* but based on entirely distinct stories – but our title is specific enough that it is likely to follow the same group of people. Even if the lost play staged a different part of the adventures of the Heraclids – or indeed a different generation of Heracles' descendants – it will have reinforced familiarity with the story and perhaps influenced the expectations of any audience members who had seen it.[13]

In addition to these general and official sources of information, Davidson (2005) reminds us to consider the informal channels through which information about the plays might have been disseminated. There were at least thirty people involved in this production, including the chorus of between twelve and fifteen,[14] the three speaking actors, the musicians, adults playing mute roles, and the children who were presumably brought to and from rehearsal by slaves, not to mention the craftspeople responsible for the costumes, masks and other material elements. We have no information about where rehearsals were held, but the performance space was outdoors with excellent sightlines; if any rehearsals at all were held in the performance space it is difficult to imagine that they were never observed. Access to this information would, of course, have been limited and privileged; nevertheless, it adds a further dimension to the audience.

We can reasonably conclude that most of the ancient audience waiting to see *Children of Heracles* would have had a general sense of the shape of the play: of the initial problem – the persecution of the children of Heracles after his death by his old enemy Eurystheus – and its resolution – that Athens would succeed in protecting them. The question is not what will happen, but how.

Outline

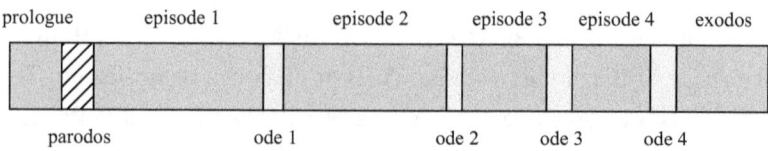

Fig. 2 Outline of the play's action.

Setting the stage

The play opens with a tableau showing a number of small boys – perhaps six of them, or as many as twelve – grouped around an altar, probably placed at or near the centre of the circular dancing area (*orchēstra*).[15] They wear the garlands and carry the branches of suppliants.[16] Near them is an old man, probably also marked as a suppliant, and behind them is the stage building (*skēnē*) representing a temple. One possible – but entirely speculative – staging is given as an aid to visualization at Figure 3.

We cannot be sure just when or how this tableau was set up. In the Greek open-air theatre there was no curtain or comparable device to conceal the actors as they took up their positions, so the actors must have arrived onstage in full view of the audience before the official start of the play in what is sometimes called a 'cancelled entry'. Perhaps a musical cue (or the absence of music) would have signalled that the audience should ignore the actors as the scene was set up.

Probable expectations established

The tableau produces a powerful visual effect, but it also allows time for speculation as to the identity of the characters onstage. For most of the audience, the children are easily identified from context, and it

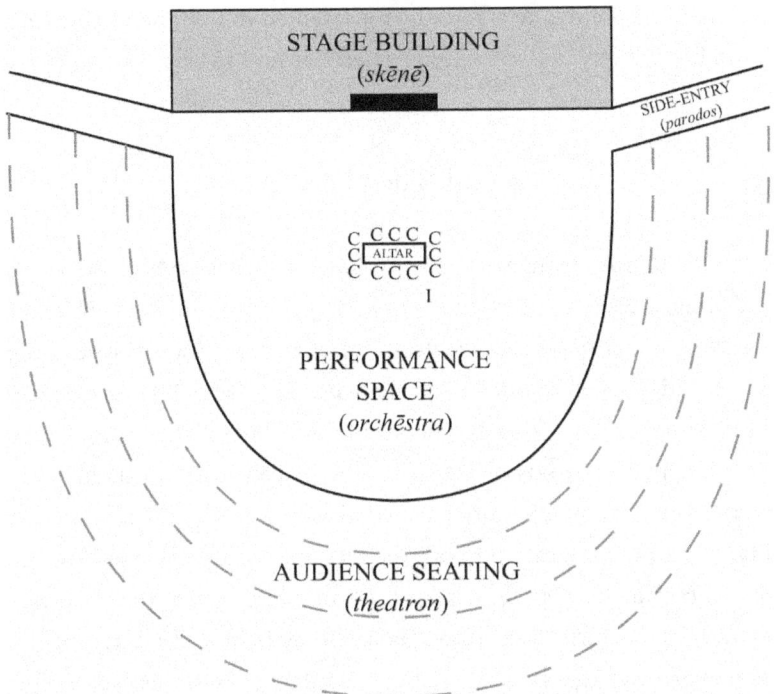

Fig. 3 Schematic of possible initial positioning, given a performance space roughly 25 metres in diameter.

will be clear from their size that they are too young to be the main chorus of the play. The white-bearded man may present something of a mystery, depending on how much information had been revealed in the *proagon*. The sight of an older man with a group of young boys might lead to the assumption that he is a tutor (*paidagōgos*), a trusted slave attendant and a common figure on the Greek stage.[17] Heracles himself is not a plausible candidate, both because the story depends on his being dead and because it would be a strange departure indeed to portray him as old. Amphitryon, Heracles' father, is possible as an old guardian for the children (and will appear in this capacity in Euripides' *Heracles*, a later play that begins with similar staging), although in various sources he does not survive until old age. Iolaus is a remote possibility; he is broadly represented in mythology as being Heracles' nephew, and we would not expect him to be so old.

Prologue (1–72)

The old man introduces himself as Iolaus and situates us in place and time: we are at Marathon, which is presented in the play as an extension of Athens despite its geographical separation (see map, Fig. 1, viii),[18] after the death of Heracles. The Heraclids have come there to seek refuge from the persecution of Eurystheus, whom they have escaped in Argos, but who has managed to drive them from every other city where they have tried to settle. The children at the altar are the youngest sons of Heracles; the older ones, led by the eldest, Hyllus, have gone in search of an alternative place of refuge should Athens turn them away. The building behind the actors is the temple of Zeus Agoraios, where the daughters of Heracles are waiting with his mother Alcmene. Iolaus emphasizes the vulnerability of the Heraclids and his own loyalty in trying to safeguard them, despite his old age, in the face of relentless persecution by Eurystheus.

His speech is interrupted by the arrival of a Herald – sometimes called Copreus for convenience[19] – marked by a distinctive staff (*kērukeion*) and perhaps a travelling cloak and hat, sent by Eurystheus from Argos. The Herald escalates the tension by forcibly grabbing Iolaus and perhaps the children, although the extent of the physical contact is difficult to establish in the absence of stage directions. Iolaus calls to the citizens for help.

Probable expectations established

The cry for help (*boē*) as a reaction to violence is a convention deeply embedded in Greek legal custom and literary culture, as is the response of a third party (called the *boēdromia*, 'running in answer to a cry,' a ritual which gave its name to a major Athenian festival and the summer month when it took place).[20] The audience is therefore primed to expect an intervention on behalf of Iolaus and the children.[21]

Entrance song of the chorus (*parodos*, 73–117)

The chorus arrives in answer to Iolaus' call for help and interrupts the Herald's attempted violence. It is likely that they place themselves between the Heraclids and the Herald.[22] They are not described as old until the next scene (120), but their age is immediately signalled by their white hair. They are sympathetic to Iolaus, and learn who the newcomers are. The Herald interrupts to demand the surrender of the children. When the chorus does not comply, he insists on speaking with the city's ruler.

The dynamic of this entrance is unusual. In most plays the chorus enters singing a lengthy song structured in pairs of verses (*strophe* and *antistrophe*) that is basically expository. In our play this song takes the form of an interview with Iolaus, and the chorus is almost entirely restricted to asking questions. The fact of their intervention is crucial, but the song focuses our attention on Iolaus, prefiguring the chorus' unusually abbreviated role throughout this play.

First episode (118–352)

The current rulers of the city are the sons of Theseus, Demophon and the silent Acamas, who now arrive (probably with attendants). The chorus describes the situation and Demophon asks the Herald to explain himself. The scene that follows is an *agon*, a set-piece debate common in Greek drama consisting of balanced speeches by characters arguing against each other, often before a 'judge' figure, and often followed by cross-examination in rapid line-by-line dialogue (called *stichomythia*).[23] This play provides a slight variant on that pattern; the Herald and Iolaus present their cases in a pair of long speeches, and after Demophon makes his decision in Iolaus' favour he takes over the old man's part in the cross-examination, and concludes by sending the Herald away in threatening terms. The Herald leaves promising to return with an army. Iolaus then delivers a long speech of thanksgiving to Demophon and Athens, promising the eternal remembrance of this favour by the Heraclids and their descendants, while the children and the chorus clasp hands. Demophon and Acamas leave; Iolaus and the children remain at the altar having refused an invitation to the palace.

It is unclear whether the children and Iolaus remove the markers of their suppliant status (the wreaths and the branches). It is possible that they do so now, or later in the play, or perhaps not at all.

First ode (*stasimon*) (353–80)

The chorus returns our focus to the Herald's threat and in a direct and unwavering song repudiates the Argive attempt at intimidation, celebrating Athens' moral and artistic superiority.

Probable expectations established

The immediate threat of the Herald is resolved, but the chorus' emphasis on the impending battle is likely to raise expectations of developments in that direction.

Second episode (381–607)

Demophon returns to the stage (apparently without Acamas, possibly with attendants) to report an alarming development. The Athenians have prepared for the arrival of the Argive army, but in the process of the customary consultation of oracles before battle he has learned that victory depends on the sacrifice of a noble virgin to Persephone. He cannot make this demand of his people, and with the Argive army at the gates he is in a difficult political situation. Iolaus offers his own life to Eurystheus, a proposal which Demophon acknowledges as noble but rejects as ineffective. At this impasse the (oldest?) Daughter of Heracles – sometimes called Macaria for convenience[24] – comes from the temple building and, when she hears of the situation, volunteers to be the sacrifice. After impassioned discussion, this offer is accepted and she leaves the stage with Demophon. Iolaus collapses in grief, is covered by his robes, and remains onstage during the following ode.

Second ode (608–29)

The chorus reflect on change as the lot of mortals; they comfort Iolaus and praise the Daughter.

Probable expectations established

Given Iolaus' grieving posture on the ground, the dedication of the second part of the ode to the virtues of the Daughter, and her own insistence on what is owed to her, we are primed to expect a continued focus on the Daughter – perhaps an account of her death.

Third episode (630–747)

The Herald[25] of Hyllus arrives with news of his master's return to Athens with the support of new allies. Alcmene is called onstage and after a brief misunderstanding the Herald delivers a short report on the military preparations. As he is about to leave for the battlefield, Iolaus unexpectedly declares his intention of participating in the battle despite his age. He rejects all attempts to dissuade him, and sends the Herald into the temple to borrow arms and armour; it is possible that this is the point at which he removes the suppliant elements of his costume. When the Herald emerges with the armour, Iolaus' physical unfitness is demonstrated as he is unable to wear or even carry it. Nevertheless, Iolaus leaves the stage for the battlefield, following the Herald with undiminished resolution. It seems very likely that Alcmene remains onstage with the children.

Third ode (748–83)

The chorus declares its readiness to fight and its faith in Athens, the gods and justice. This is the longest of the play's short odes, collapsing the time required for battle.

Probable expectations established

We expect a report of the battle. The mythological tradition makes us confident that Athens and the Heraclids will win, and other accounts (admittedly mostly late) state that Eurystheus is killed and beheaded by either Hyllus or Iolaus.[26] However, it is uncertain whether the rejuvenation of Iolaus could be anticipated by a fifth-century audience, as there is no account of this transformation that predates our play.[27]

Fourth episode (784–891)

A slave of the Heraclids arrives announcing that Athens has been victorious. Alcmene grants freedom to the Slave in gratitude for this information, to which he adds the news that Iolaus has not only survived but has been miraculously rejuvenated. He then delivers a long narrative account of the battle in a familiar set-piece known as a 'messenger speech.'[28] Hyllus challenged Eurystheus to decide the battle in single combat, but the challenge was not accepted. In the battle that followed, the Athenian army defeated the Argives. The Slave has also heard that Iolaus' prayer for youth was miraculously fulfilled and that he captured Eurystheus as he was fleeing after his army's defeat. Eurystheus will soon be brought to Alcmene for punishment. The Slave leaves, while Alcmene (in all probability) remains onstage.

Fourth ode (892–927)

The chorus celebrates the victory and Athens.

Probable expectations established

We expect the arrival of the defeated and unwilling Eurystheus (883–7), accompanied at least by the rejuvenated Iolaus (861–3). We may also speculate about the possible return of Demophon (and Acamas), and perhaps also the first appearance of Hyllus.

Exodos (928–1055)

Hyllus' Herald returns to the stage with Eurystheus, and announces that Iolaus and Hyllus are still at the battlefield honouring Zeus (936–8).

Alcmene taunts her old enemy and declares her intention of killing him. Unexpectedly, she learns that this has been forbidden by the Athenian leaders. Alcmene repeats her intention. Eurystheus refuses to plead for his life and explains the rationale for his treatment of the Heraclids; he had persecuted Heracles at Hera's command, and after the hero's death his enemy could not allow children who hated him to grow up and take revenge on him. The chorus advises Alcmene to obey the Athenians, but she comes up with a compromise strategy: she will kill him but will return his body to his people. Unexpectedly Eurystheus himself embraces this. He reveals a prophecy received from Apollo: that he will be buried at Pallene (in Attica) and will serve as a protector hero for Athens, and in the future will help them against an invasion by the descendants of the Heraclids. Alcmene urges the chorus to comply, and . . .

The ending

In the text as we have it, the chorus is fully persuaded. In the closing lines of the play they give Alcmene permission to kill Eurystheus despite the explicit prohibition relayed by Hyllus' Herald, saying: 'This seems right to me. Go on, servants, for we consider that our deeds[29] will leave the kings clean' (1053–5). Everyone leaves the stage.

There are two significant difficulties that may strike us. The first is Alcmene's willingness to violate the Athenian decree protecting Eurystheus in order to secure her revenge against him. Her ferocity is not in itself surprising; revenge is common and forgiveness rare in tragedy, and maternal revenge is a pointed and problematic subset that encompasses figures from Hecuba to Clytemnestra.[30] Many plays present us with the deliberate destruction of loved ones or former loved ones, but in our case the identity of the victim causes no moral difficulties; Alcmene's anger against the man who has implacably persecuted her family is 'terrible, yet forgivable' (981), as the chorus says. It is also in keeping with her earlier characterization. Alcmene's first scene has shown her to be resolute in a position of vulnerability; it is consistent for her to be equally uncompromising in her new position of power. Burnett goes so far as to frame her actions as essentially admirable and satisfying to a Greek audience, arguing that, like the Daughter, she is a woman taking positive action in the place of men paralysed by their own institutions (1976: 21–6, 1998: 151–6), and benefitting Athens by her action.

Yet Euripides invites the audience to take a more critical look at Alcmene's actions by emphasizing the parallels between the Heraclids' initial position and Eurystheus' final one.[31] Both are threatened by a powerful enemy, dependent on Athenian goodwill for survival, and physically vulnerable in the absence of an active party to enact or enforce that goodwill. The Heraclids were dependent on the widespread Greek convention (*nomos*) protecting suppliants at an altar; Eurystheus is dependent on a similar custom protecting prisoners of war (as we will see in Chapter 4). Euripides emphasizes it in his play as endorsed by the Athenian leaders in particular (961–6), accepted by Hyllus in this specific case (967–8), and also (if Eurystheus is to be believed) by the Greeks in general (1008–12). Alcmene's disregard for this convention is therefore not only a betrayal of the decision and principles of her protectors, but it is also specifically likened to the impious behaviour of Eurystheus' Herald in the prologue and his pointedly offensive disregard for Athenian independence. The solution that she proposes – that if she kills Eurystheus but releases his body for burial she can avoid violating the city's ruling (1020–5) – is similar in nature to but even less convincing than the sophistic suggestions made earlier by the Herald, who argued that taking the Heraclids by force reflects badly on the Herald, but not on the Athenians, and that he will not have to drag them away if the Athenians will only put them out of their city

(252–8). Alcmene is presented in this final scene not as merely vengeful; she shares the Argive Herald's *hubris*.[32]

More difficult still is the problem of the chorus' reaction. Their king firmly rejected the Herald's letter-of-the-law suggestions as foolish attempts to trick the gods (258), and they themselves later spoke up to restrain the agitated Demophon from violating the sacrosanctity of the herald (273 and perhaps 271); but now the chorus endorses Alcmene's plan to kill Eurystheus. This response is not entirely unprepared. At 1018–19 they advise Alcmene against exacting her revenge, but at 1020–1 they have already welcomed the possibility of any solution that will allow Alcmene to carry out her revenge while also 'obeying the city.' When Alcmene makes her proposal, the chorus' response is initially forestalled by Eurystheus, who accepts death and adds an incentive for the city to allow it by telling of the prophesized benefits that his death will bring. They are not able to reply directly to him either; Alcmene seizes the opportunity to urge the chorus once more to accept her plan. When the chorus is finally allowed to speak, the explanation given for their decision is minimal and negative rather than positive – not giving a rationale for permitting the death, but noting the absence of a particular consequence. It is accordingly unclear whether the chorus is persuaded or simply overmastered into accepting the inevitable.

An easy solution is to blame a faulty text[33] – to assume that some lines have been lost that contained a resolution to this situation: a literal or figurative *deus ex machina* arriving to take charge of the ending, since none of the characters onstage has the authority to persuade or overrule Alcmene. This, however, is a potentially dangerous solution. It is true that all texts from antiquity are vulnerable, particularly those, like this play, which depend on a single manuscript copied and recopied over centuries. Many of our texts show signs of alteration, both deliberate and accidental, from whole scenes to single letters, and textual criticism is the branch of scholarship whose business it is to identify and address these issues. However, it is dangerous to assume that what we find subjectively difficult is objectively faulty, and we must consider whether there is any evidence for a problem with the text.

At the level of detail, there is no difficulty with the text as transmitted, either grammatically or in terms of literal meaning; it is only the interpretation that has caused trouble. The brevity of the chorus' statement is in keeping with the typical style of Euripidean closing choral lines. But there are two larger-scale facts that we can consider. The first is that this play is some 300 lines (almost a quarter) shorter than the average extant Euripidean play. The second is that there are a handful of fragments quoted by other authors as being from Euripides' *Children of Heracles*, but which do not appear in the manuscript texts of our play. (These are provided in the appendix of this book.) At first glance it seems plausible to take these as signs that an important scene may have been lost from somewhere in our text. However, this supposition does not hold up to scrutiny either for the play in general or for the closing sequence in particular.

No episode of our play, including this final scene, is noticeably short. It is possible that something significant may have dropped out,[34] but the brevity of *Children of Heracles* as a whole does not increase the likelihood of a significant loss of text in any episode. Furthermore, while there is no Euripidean play of comparable length, Aeschylus' *Choephoroi* is only twenty lines longer than our play. Similarly, it is possible that the orphaned fragments have indeed come from our play, although attributions of this kind are not entirely reliable and many scholars now agree that these fragments do not belong to our play. But even if we accept that they belong somewhere in *Children of Heracles*, it is difficult to fit any of them into this final scene; the content of the fragments – three focusing on the obligations of children to their parents, one comparing the benefits of being a sacrifice and of staying alive, and one about confusion – does not fit into a scene in which an alternative to Alcmene's revenge is proposed and adopted.

The evidence for a missing scene is circumstantial at best. We must therefore be prepared to accept and account for the unsettling nature of Alcmene's vengeance and of the chorus' acceptance of it as we consider our interpretation of the play as a whole.

Summing the Parts

Many tragedies – though by no means all – follow a straightforward decline in the fortunes of a central figure or figures. *Children of Heracles* apparently follows the reverse pattern; the collective 'hero' begins the play in a position of vulnerability and despair, and ends the play in general security and specific triumph over its primary enemy. This outline, however, does not capture the complexity of the play's structure.

The aim of this chapter is to suggest three ways in which we can set the scenes in relation to each other and frame the action of the play as a whole. Choosing a different focal point – the Heraclids themselves, their relationship with Athens, the expectations of an experienced audience – yields a different framework. None of these has any particular claim to authority, nor are they mutually exclusive; different readers will find different patterns useful just as the individual members of the Greek audience would have done. I offer these three as examples of how we can understand the swift and constant changes in the play not as disorienting but as a principle of Euripides' construction.

(a) The Heraclids

The first proposed framework focuses on the collective circumstances and characterization of the Heraclids.[1] This structures the play into two halves, with the first part of the play centred on the physical danger faced by the Heraclids as a whole (including their guardians

Alcmene and Iolaus), and the second focused on the lifting of that external danger and the introduction of an internal ethical danger. The transition between the two halves takes place in the central scene (third episode) that introduces Alcmene and sends Iolaus offstage, and the progress of the pattern is marked for the audience by the many parallels between the prologue (focused on the arrival of Eurystheus' Herald), the central scene (focused on the arrival of Hyllus' Herald), and the exodos (focused on the arrival of Eurystheus himself, accompanied by Hyllus' Herald). The pattern is a simple but striking one.

The prologue begins with the Heraclids in great physical danger, as Iolaus repeatedly emphasizes. Their moral position is unassailable; they have committed no wrongs and are being unjustly persecuted, driven not only from Argos but from other cities in which they have sought refuge. The arrival of Eurystheus' bullying Herald both demonstrates the extent of the physical threat and entrenches the Heraclids' moral position by contrast with the Herald's brash impiety. The immediate physical threat is checked through the intervention first of the chorus and then of Demophon and Acamas, but we are reminded that the danger is magnified rather than mitigated as the Argive army approaches.

The Heraclid position becomes acute once more in the following episode as Demophon reveals the prophecy demanding a sacrifice, and the Athenian support is threatened. Once again the immediate threat is checked, this time by the self-sacrifice of the Daughter, who eliminates the latest danger to her family's physical safety at the cost of her life. At the same time, she elevates their moral position; the emphasis on the nobility of her inherited nature as the root of her action encourages the audience to generalize the credit for this action to include the Heraclids as a family.

When Hyllus' Herald opens the next episode with the news of Hyllus' arrival with military allies, both the practical and apparent moral positions of the Heraclids continue to improve. There are three marked stages in the interlinked strengthening of their position. First, Alcmene's mistaken identification of the new arrival as a renewal of the Argive threat (646–53) invites comparison with the opening of the play, which both emphasizes the change in the Heraclid fortunes since the prologue, and introduces Alcmene as Iolaus' equal in courage. Next, the news of the arrival of Hyllus' forces (664–73) not only increases the likelihood of military victory, but also changes the Heraclid identity; it is now extended from the women in the temple and the old man and the children at the altar to include the young men on the battlefield commanding their own troops. Finally, we come to Iolaus' insistence on joining the battle, seizing the sudden opportunity to join the offstage adult male Heraclids in playing an active role (680–1, 709–16). This action defies simple interpretation, as the incongruity between Iolaus' unyielding resolution and his physical weakness is likely to have provoked a range of responses. We shall return to this shortly. For now, the Heraclids are shown to be partners on equal footing with the Athenians in the battle to come; everyone, from the young woman to the old man, is prepared to share the risks. This is the climax of the Heraclids' position; they and their allies are poised for military victory, and they have proven their innocence, piety and courage, with every individual given the opportunity to show the same sterling qualities.

From this point, the material fortunes of the Heraclids are assured by offstage events. The battle is won; Iolaus is miraculously rejuvenated; Eurystheus is captured. The final scene, which presents Eurystheus at Alcmene's mercy, shows the complete inversion of their initial positions. Yet this inversion includes their moral positions as well as their fortunes. Alcmene's implacable vengeance in defiance of Athenian law can be read as the culmination of an unsettling undercurrent in the presentation of the Heraclids that first shows itself in the pivotal central scene.

These first hints are subtle, and are introduced through that most effective and subversive of techniques: comedy. In the central scene, Alcmene's first appearance and Iolaus' last, Euripides plays with comic touches that lend an edge of foolishness to both of the older heroes; they are both absolutely in earnest and their intentions are irreproachable, but the incongruity of their reactions to events is increasingly emphasized. Alcmene's first entrance is marked by error; she has misread the situation and has arrived onstage prepared for conflict in a situation calling for joy. It is impossible to gauge just how far this incongruity descends into absurdity; much depends on how this scene is performed, and this information – the body language and tones of voice – are lost to us. In a varied audience there may well have been some spectators who found this scene genuinely funny. But there is nothing in the responses of her internal audience to invite laughter or mockery or even pity for her error rather than admiration of her spirit.

We cannot say the same of Iolaus' insistence on joining the battle. When he first declares his intentions the Herald is barely polite ('It is unlike you to say something so stupid', 682), the chorus is incredulous ('Why do you struggle uselessly like this?' 704), and Alcmene's reproaches are unsympathetic ('What's this? Are you out of your mind?' 709). His exchanges with the Herald are particularly undermining, drawing from tropes familiar to us from later comedy. In the disagreement between a social superior and a more sensible subordinate we can recognize the 'clever slave' and the master of Roman Comedy, or Sancho Panza and Don Quixote, or Jeeves and Wooster. The old man's refusal to accept the limitations of reality and his belief in his physical strength and imagined exploits suggest a pathetic kind of *miles gloriosus* ('swaggering soldier'),[2] while the dialogue of the Herald's protests and Iolaus' responses borders on cross-talk banter. All of these elements resonate with comedy, though none is explicitly developed;

neither action nor language is comedic here, but the dynamics of the exchange are.

This dynamic intensifies in the second part of the scene when the Herald returns with the armour, and Euripides stages at some length the grotesque spectacle of Iolaus' pathetic attempts to play the part of a young man. The play proceeds on the edge of physical comedy as Iolaus leans on the Herald's arm and urges him to hurry without realizing his own slowness. The nobility of Iolaus' intentions remains unchallenged, but the scene undermines his tragic stature, and tests the limits of our sympathy with his intentions under the pressure of ridicule.

In the following scene, the main battle narrative itself is unambiguously positive; in particular Hyllus' challenge and Iolaus' miraculous transformation are presented in a very favourable light. The speech itself, however, is framed by a peculiar detail: Alcmene reacts to the first declaration of the victory by freeing the slave who brings the news (788–9). This may strike us simply as a measure of her joy, and various figures in tragedy bring good news expecting a reward (e.g. the Corinthian at *OT* 1005–6, the Trachinian at *Trach.* 190–1). However, to a Greek audience Alcmene's action may have struck a strange chord. The freeing (manumission) of slaves was not uncommon, but it is no mere romantic gesture, nor would it have been as unambiguously positive for Euripides' spectators as it is for a modern audience.[3] In a slaveholding culture, manumission is a significant economic decision that affects a family's wealth, and records from the Greek world of the fifth century – though not specifically from Athens – show awareness of this ramification.[4] What is more, in the fifth century it was unusual for a woman to free any slave,[5] let alone one with a military function, and in the preceding scene Alcmene has already emphatically disengaged herself from the military proceedings (665), and Iolaus has reinforced this dissociation (711). When Alcmene, an old woman, frees a man fresh from the battlefield without the consent of her family, she can be seen to be exercising an authority to which she does not have a right.

If so, this scene anticipates her explicit and unsettling overreaching of authority in the final scene. Onstage, Eurystheus invites comparison with the other figures in the play who have courageously faced danger and death: Iolaus in the prologue, the Daughter in her sacrifice scene, and Alcmene in her mistaken belief that the Argives have returned. We may not fully accept his shifting of the responsibility to Hera (989–90), or his presentation of the persecution of the Heraclids as a reasonable precaution (1000–8), but Eurystheus is certainly presented as a man accepting of his fate and calm in defeat, acknowledging the mercy intended by the Athenians despite Alcmene's overriding actions (1027–30).

The more positively Eurystheus is perceived – and this degree will vary depending on the audience member[6] – the more Alcmene's revenge appears morally compromised. To her determination to subvert the Athenians' decree Eurystheus then adds the prediction of the ingratitude of the Heraclids' descendants (1032–7), a piercing intrusion of the political situation of Euripides' time into the mythic plot, as we will shortly see in greater detail. The audience is therefore encouraged to frame Alcmene's betrayal of Athenian principles not only as the action of an individual, stereotypical or otherwise,[7] but also in the context of this broader Heraclid betrayal of the Athenians themselves.

This framework yields a dark reading of the play as a whole: the Heraclids are sympathetic as victims, but when they achieve safety and power they show the same *hubris* as their persecutor, disregarding both the claims of the victim and the decrees of Athens. Not even the Athenians come out unscathed – the final complicity of the chorus implicates them too in a short-sighted and underhanded *Realpolitik* that undermines the loftier ideals of the Athenian rulers.

(b) The relationship of the Heraclids with Athens

By following not the fortunes of the Heraclids themselves but the quality of their changing relationship with Athens, we can see the play as a series of harmonies and dissonances. This may seem a less intuitive focus to a modern audience, but there was a very specific reason for Euripides' audience to notice and respond to this dynamic: this play, like every other Euripidean play, was performed during tensions between Athens and Sparta that culminated in the two Peloponnesian wars (460–445 and 431–404). The Spartans were explicitly identified as early as the seventh *c.* BCE – by both the Spartan poet Tyrtaeus and non-Spartan sources such as Pindar – as the descendants of the Heraclids; their dual royal houses traced their lineage back to Eurysthenes and Procles, legendary Heraclid twins who became the first kings of Sparta after their father died leading the final and successful invasion of the Peloponnese and fulfilling the prophecy of the Heraclid return.[8]

Dealing as it does with the diplomatic relations between two city-states that were in conflict at the time of the play's production, this reading necessarily has political implications.[9] However, for the moment we will focus primarily on the relationships presented within the play itself and their probable resonance at any point in the second half of the fifth century – that is to say, the general context of conflict between Athens and Sparta; in Chapter 5 we will take a closer look at the range of possible specific historical contexts and their importance to our interpretation of the play. This reading can become more elaborate if we consider additional factors, such as the role of Argos (a traditional competitor with Sparta for dominance in the Peloponnese and an ally of Athens to a greater or lesser extent during Euripides' lifetime) and the extent to which the citizen-bodies (Athenians and Argives) are treated as distinct from their rulers (Demophon/Acamas and Eurystheus).

The play begins with the Heraclids waiting at the altar to present their case for sanctuary to the Athenian kings; in modern terms they are asylum seekers without refugee status. Iolaus is hopeful, pointing not to the reputation of Athens but the claims of personal kinship (*genos*) between the Heraclids and the children of Theseus (38–9). This claim is attacked by the Argive Herald, who stresses their civic rather than kinship identity, pointing out to Demophon in the first episode that the Heraclids are not Athenians but Argives (139–43). In addition to contrasting Heraclid and Athenian interests, he frames the public interest of the city and Demophon's personal interests (concerning his own position in the eyes of his citizens) as distinct but aligned (166). Iolaus rejects the first argument, claiming that as fugitives the Heraclids can no longer be considered Argives (185–9), but makes use of the Herald's distinction between Athens and Demophon, combining praise for the city (192–201) with a lengthy reminder of the family and personal obligations of Theseus to Heracles (205–19). By adding personal supplication (grasping Demophon's knees and chin, 226–7) to the supplication at the public altar, he counters the Herald's threat of public and personal danger with the pressure of public and personal disgrace. In deciding to support Iolaus' claim, Demophon emphasizes the personal rather than the public angle: after his respect for the altar of Zeus, he is motivated by the obligations of kinship, and finally the fear of personal dishonour if it were thought that Athens is afraid of Argos (236–46). This scene establishes the Heraclids as refugees; more importantly for this framework it aligns Athenian and Heraclid interests, as well as personal and public interests for Demophon and the Athenians. The routing of the impious Herald suggests that this is an appropriate and satisfying decision.

This alignment of interests is apparently confirmed after the Herald's exit as Iolaus delivers a lengthy speech of gratitude. He begins with a praise of nobility, praise that in its generality encompasses both the sons of Theseus and the children of Heracles. He then instructs the children to take the hands of the old men of the chorus. We cannot know the details of this movement, but physical contact is relatively rare on the Greek stage, and contact between the chorus and actors rarer still.[10] What is more, the movement of two large groups of figures is a striking piece of staging, enhanced by the contrast between the old men and the young boys. The physical contact between the two groups is a powerful visual symbol of the alliance between the Heraclids and the people of Marathon and Athens. Iolaus concludes his speech by praising Demophon as worthy of his father Theseus. Demophon accepts this, and before leaving to prepare for the Argive invasion he invites Iolaus and the children to leave the altar and enter his home (*domous*, 340–3). Iolaus declines, maintaining the distinction of Heraclid identity;[11] however, he confirms the merging of their interests as he redefines the focus of the supplication from personal to public. The children are now suppliants not for their own protection but 'for the well-being of the city,' and will leave the altar when the new threat to Athens is resolved (344–6).

But there is a pointed undercurrent to this apparent confirmation of the two alliances – of Heraclid and Athenian, personal and public interests – achieved during the confrontation with the Argive Herald. While the chorus and the children are clasping hands, Iolaus tells the Heraclids never to 'raise spears in war against this land' (314). When Demophon replies to Iolaus' speech, he states that he is confident that 'the favour will be remembered' (334). To Euripides' audience, watching this play in the context of the Spartan invasions of Attica, the ominous undercurrent is obvious, and the irony is no less powerful for its anachronism.

Within the world of the play, however, the Athenian-Heraclid alliance is faced by the new challenge presented by the divine demand for a sacrifice. The Argive Herald, unsympathetic as he is, is proved to have been right in the two threatening predictions he made (158–68); the city is now under attack, and Demophon's position in the eyes of his citizens is at risk (415–24). This is a serious threat to Heraclid safety, to their relationship with the Athenians, and perhaps also to Athens' own self-image.[12] Demophon's wording is diplomatic, but as Iolaus puts it, he 'says not explicitly, but says anyway' (494) that the Heraclids are at risk of being sent away from Athens. However, this anxiety does not last for long; in the very next speech the Daughter of Heracles resolves the dilemma by offering herself as the victim. This action instantly reinstates the Heraclid-Athenian relationship, not only demonstrating the nobility of the Heraclids and their worthiness of Athenian protection, but also uniting Demophon, Iolaus and the chorus in praising the Daughter.

Important as the Daughter's sacrifice is, the nature of the relationship between the Heraclids and the Athenians in the play is more materially shifted by the news of Hyllus' return in the next scene. He brings a large number of reinforcements (664–9) – although we learn no details about where they have come from or why they have joined Hyllus – and he is stationed on the Athenians' left wing (671) as they prepare to go into battle. Athenian protection is still accepted and appreciated (715–16), but the Heraclids are no longer dependent refugees in Athens; they are active allies.

There is also a short passage that might have deepened the resonance of this scene for some members of Euripides' audience. As Iolaus leaves the stage to join the battle after his pointed exchange with Hyllus' Herald, he reminds the audience that once he and Heracles captured Sparta (741–2). This refers to a relatively obscure adventure of Heracles' in which he kills Hippocoon, the brother and supplanter of Tyndareus, the king of Sparta. Our other sources for this adventure are all late (second *c.* CE);[13] none of them mentions Iolaus, and Heracles' motives are purely personal, focused on his hatred of Hippocoon and his sons. By referring to this adventure at this point in the action and focusing on the city instead of its ruler, Euripides seems to be deliberately setting up Iolaus and Heracles as enemies of Sparta, temporarily displacing the usual tradition that associates Sparta with

Heraclid ancestry. It is even possible that an audience would hear another anachronistic undertone to Iolaus' parting words; as he decries the popular association of prosperity with a 'reputation for courage' (746), we may hear a dig at the famous Spartan military reputation. If this is the case, it further emphasizes the impression of harmony between the Heraclids and the Athenians as equal allies united against a common enemy, with no distinction made between individual and common interests.

This last point is particularly important, because as Hyllus re-emerges into the story Demophon disappears – not only from the stage, but also from the narrative.[14] We hear of the 'lord of the Athenians' (824) addressing his 'fellow citizens' (826), but otherwise the characters now refer to the 'foremost of the Athenians' (670), '[free] men and a free city' (957), or the 'land's leaders' (964) – all terms with democratic resonance. In the last ode the chorus draws an analogy between Athena's legendary assistance to Heracles and the present salvation that 'her city and people' have offered to the Heraclids (919–25). In the final scene reference is made almost exclusively to the will of 'the land' (*chthon*, e.g. 968, 1024) or 'the city' (*polis*, 975, 1012, 1019, 1020, 1026, 1032, 1045), not of its two rulers. Not until the very last word of the play – 'the kings' (*basileusin*) – does Euripides specifically remind us of Demophon and Acamas.

The effects are subtle but important, shifting the focus onto a collective identity in place of a focal Athenian figure. The Heraclid slave reporting on the battle presents the victory as 'ours' (786), and describes a joint effort between Hyllus and the Athenians. Hyllus takes the initiative in challenging Eurystheus to leave Athens out of their dispute (805), but when the Argive king refuses the focus shifts to the Athenians as a collective, and the emphasis is on the efforts of the troops until the Argives are routed (819–42). Hyllus' troops are not specifically mentioned; there is no differentiation between these reinforcements and the Athenians. The Heraclid presence then comes to the foreground again through Iolaus (843–66), giving the battle narrative a neat structure with an individual Heraclid focus bookending the collective efforts of the armies. What is more, the culmination of the pursuit of Eurystheus at the Skironian cliffs puts Iolaus in the footsteps of the legendary Athenian king Theseus, as the place was named for an enemy defeated by Theseus at that spot.[15] This association pushes Demophon further from the centre of Athenian identity in the play.

Accordingly, the surprising declaration that Alcmene must not kill Eurystheus is not presented as the decree of Demophon. We are initially told: 'it is not permitted for you to kill this man' (961), and then that 'it is not deemed right by the leaders of this land' (963).[16] Alcmene's refusal to abide by the Athenian law relayed by the Herald jeopardizes the relationship between the Heraclids and Athenians. She recognizes the importance of the alliance, declaring: 'I love (*philō*) this city; this cannot be contradicted' (975), but absolutely refuses to spare Eurystheus. This clash between Athenian practice and Alcmene's revenge is then put under still more pressure by Eurystheus' intervention. After defending his persecution of the Heraclids, he points out that killing him now in cold blood will bring pollution on his killer (1009–17) since 'the city spared me, showing restraint, honouring the gods far more than their enmity toward me' (1012–13).[17] Eurystheus highlights here not a conflict between Heraclid and Athenian interests or actions, but the ethical and religious distance between Alcmene and Athens. This point is not addressed directly, but tacitly conceded as the play continues; when the chorus diffidently tries again to persuade Alcmene to give in, she claims that she will not be disobeying the city if she returns Eurystheus' body to his friends (*philoi*) after killing him (1023).

As they seem to be on the point of resolving this conflict, Eurystheus interjects again, this time with the startling news of Apollo's prophecy. This speech explicitly reconfigures the relationships between the three parties; the former Argive king will become a benevolent Athenian metic[18] and cultic hero, and the descendants of the Heraclids will return to Athens as invaders. The language of enmity has been intensifying between Eurystheus and the Heraclids throughout the exodos; the word *echthros* (enemy) is used at lines 940, 944, 965, 996, 998, 1002, 1006, 1013 and 1049, while Eurystheus now reveals that the Athenians will be the *philoi* (friends) who will take care of his body. The language remains subtle; the word *echthros* is not directly applied to the future Athenian-Heraclid relationship, nor *philos* to Eurystheus' relationship to Athens. The dominant focus is still the enmity between Eurystheus and the Heraclids.[19]

Eurystheus' second speech also aligns Alcmene's impiety in killing him with the future Heraclid betrayal of the promise of gratitude made to the chorus and Demophon at 314–44. We can no longer confine the problems of the exodos to Alcmene as an individual, but are encouraged to see her action as part of a wider pattern of betrayal. The core of this speech is not a plea for Eurystheus' life or even a defence of his actions, but a demonstration of the conflict of long-term Athenian and Heraclid interests and, through the connection of current and future betrayals, the attribution of the responsibility to Heraclid nature: 'this is the kind of foreigner you have sponsored' (1036–7). Our awareness of the two timeframes – the mythical and the contemporary – becomes acute, and the conflict over Eurystheus' death gains both depth and immediacy for the Athenian audience.

In addition to this, we may consider some possible implications of the new positioning of Eurystheus as Athens' ally for the portrayal of Argos. In the first scene, the city is associated through Eurystheus' Herald with tyranny and *hubris* (134–46); however, there is a persistent and not unflattering emphasis put on their military power throughout the play. This is not limited to the Argive Herald's own claims (e.g. 175–83), but includes the respect shown by the chorus, who recognize that 'the Ares [i.e. martial power] of the Myceneans is very fierce' (290), and sing that 'it is terrible that the prosperous city of Mycenae, very famous for the might of the spear, should nurse wrath against my city' (159–62). Demophon likewise states that 'every man at Argos is a quick ally (*boēdromos*)' (39), a word that is also used to describe the kind of assistance that the chorus brings to Iolaus in the opening scene (see pp. 8–9 above). The Slave's balanced description of the battle itself (830–40) also presents the Argives as – almost – the martial equals of the Athenians. All this may well be simply part of the construction of the plight of the Heraclids and the valour of the Athenians, but in the context of fifth-century diplomatic relations it may have greater weight. Argos was Sparta's traditional rival in the Peloponnese and one of Athens' primary allies in the first Peloponnesian War, starting in 460 when (with Athenian help) the Argives rejected Spartan control. In this context, Eurystheus' new alliance with Athens may resonate with contemporary views of Argos – not a leader to follow, but a valuable ally.[20]

We are given little time to process these shifts as the play draws rapidly to a close. Alcmene manages to have her cake and eat it too; far from challenging Eurystheus' framing of the situation she embraces it as an incentive for Athens to approve of her present plan, urging the chorus – the only party that might interfere – to accept his killing as the 'safest course' (1048), since his death brings benefit (1049). In doing so she tacitly accepts his forecast of future enmity between the Heraclids and Athens and uses this to persuade the chorus to capitulate in the present conflict between their priorities, while relying on the alliance built up over the course of the play to continue to frame Eurystheus as the enemy (*echthros*, 1049). The chorus' final lines reflect this acceptance: by allowing Alcmene to incur pollution and protecting the religious purity of their kings (just as they earlier intervened to prevent Demophon from violating the sanctity of the Argive Herald, 270–2), the chorus accepts the division of Athenian and Heraclid interests, and rejects Athenian responsibility for the Heraclids and their actions.

This framework sees the play end in an ambiguous situation, both resolved and unresolved. The Heraclids and the Athenians are apparently both in harmony and also in conflict, while the audience's focus is explicitly divided between short-term and long-term perspectives.

(c) Plot types

The third framework focuses on a particular set of expectations, attempting to reconstruct the experience of an audience member who had seen many plays and was familiar with a range of plot devices and conventions – that is to say, a spectator with some of the qualities shared by modern readers and students of tragedy. Earlier (pp. 4–5 above) we touched on the possible role of Aeschylus' lost *Children of Heracles* in shaping the audience's familiarity with the relevant mythology. The third framework broadens this idea to consider the context provided by plays that do not follow the same specific plot or even the same broad branch of mythology, but that present similar story patterns. Traditional narratives of all kinds tend to depend on types and motifs; correspondingly, tragedy uses a number of 'recurrent roles and situations' (Taplin 1977: 192; cf. Dubischar 2017: 374–7). These patterns will have been familiar to those spectators who had seen a large number of plays – the same spectators who would appreciate Homeric allusions and especially the parodies of tragedy so often found in comedy. When we consider the plot of *Children of Heracles* in this light we can trace a quick alternation of such patterns.

This framework depends on two assumptions. First, it presupposes that a substantial subset of the audience was familiar with a number of other tragedies – not an unlikely supposition given the regular attendance of most Athenians at the annual performances, ensured both by the inherent popularity of the genre and by the festival context of the dramatic competitions. Indeed, it is more reasonable to suppose that an experienced audience member would recognize a general pattern than a specific allusion to a particular play. A more fraught question is whether we can reasonably use the evidence from later plays to extrapolate background patterns for a relatively early play like *Children of Heracles*. None of Euripides' earliest work has survived intact. Only two of Sophocles' seven extant plays can be securely dated at all and both were performed after our play, in the last decade of the fifth century. Given the uncertainty of the dating of our play (see pp. 87–91 below), it is possible but unprovable (and in my opinion unlikely) that one or more of the others predates *Children of Heracles*. Since only Aeschylus and a very few fragmentary plays can be confidently taken as precedent, we cannot say with certainty how conventional the audience would have found any of the scenes of *Children of Heracles*. Nevertheless, we know that Euripides gained a reputation for being conscious and critical of poetry in general and of his predecessors in particular.[21] I am therefore ready to assume a recognizable convention where we find a plot sequence that is common in later Euripides and that appears at least once in the plays that likely predate our play.

Working from this premise, we can read *Children of Heracles* as a sequence of four different patterns that would have been recognized by an experienced audience member: a supplication, a sacrifice, a battle and a revenge. This is not to say that Euripides is alluding to any specific plays, nor that his intent was to produce a metatheatrical or satirical pastiche of the genre, or a metapoetic tour *à la* James Joyce's *Ulysses*. I simply suggest that the play's heterogeneous nature is deliberate, its pace compressed and accelerated, and its structure dependent on the interplay of familiarity, change and surprise.

The suppliant pattern tends to include the following elements: a vulnerable individual or group (often with a male spokesman, regardless of the identity of the group) seeking refuge at an altar; the

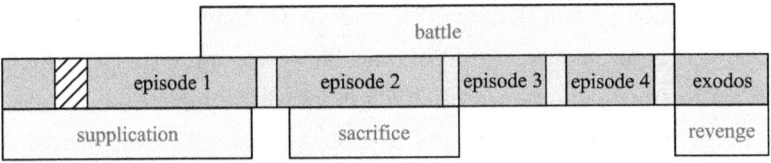

Fig. 4 Outline of plot patterns.

arrival of the persecutor; a call for help; the arrival of a protector who rescues the victim from the immediate threat.[22] This sequence would certainly have been familiar to those audience members who had been present at Aeschylus' *Suppliant Women* or *Eumenides*, as it makes up the majority of the action of these plays. The elements of this sequence are also used on a smaller scale in many other tragedies. A suppliant tableau opens Sophocles' *Oedipus Tyrannos*, and after using it in our play Euripides would return to it in subsequent plays including *Heracles, Andromache, Suppliant Women* and *Helen*. The arrival of an aggressor is paralleled in most of these examples, from Aeschylus' Egyptian Herald (*Supp.* 825) and Clytemnestra's Ghost (*Eum.* 94) to Lycus (*Her.* 139) and Menelaus (*And.* 309). The (attempted) seizure of a vulnerable person is a common situation in tragedy, not limited to suppliants at the altar but including defenceless people such as the wounded Philoctetes (*Phil.* 985–1008), the girl Antigone (*Oedipus at Colonus* 826–47), and the blind and old Oedipus (*OC* 859–83). It is also one of the most intense and suspenseful interactions between characters in a genre that generally avoids the staging of violent conflict, and usually occurs at a climactic moment toward the end of the suppliant pattern. By introducing the villainous Argive Herald near the very beginning of the play, Euripides thrusts the audience of *Children of Heracles* into the thick of an immediate crisis, drastically accelerating the usual pace of this sequence. Iolaus' cry for help produces the expected effect of bringing rescue. This role, paralleled by intervening figures such as Pelasgus in

Aeschylus' *Suppliant Women,* Theseus in *Oedipus at Colonus,* and
Peleus in *Andromache,* is split in our play between the chorus, which
interrupts the abduction, and Demophon, who completes the rescue
and sends the aggressor away. The suppliant pattern is resolved, and
the meaning of the children's presence at the altar is explicitly shifted
(344–6).

Children of Heracles accordingly gives us a typical pattern with
Iolaus and the Heraclids as suppliants, the Argive Herald as persecutor,
and Demophon as protector, but compresses it into perhaps half of its
usual space. Few plays focus entirely on a suppliant dilemma; most
suppliant patterns introduce a second substantial development, such
as the threat to Athens by the Furies in *Eumenides* (beginning at
778, three quarters of the way through the play), the madness of
Heracles in *Heracles Furens* (beginning at line 815 of 1428), or the
remorse of Hermione in *Andromache* (beginning at line 802 of 1288).
Nevertheless, in these cases the suppliant pattern focuses the action
for more than half of the play, while ours is completed at the end of
the first episode. It is remarkable in two other respects. First, it is
presented with astonishing ethical simplicity. There is no ambiguity
or hesitation in either Demophon's or the audience's judgement of
the Argive and Heraclid claims.[23] Secondly, our play connects the
suppliant pattern more closely to the remainder of the play by the
simple expedient of leaving the children onstage at the altar. Though
the suppliant plot resolves, the suppliant tableau lingers.[24]

The second pattern to emerge is a battle sequence which includes
the next three episodes. This is one of the less common patterns in our
extant plays, but it includes Aeschylus' *Seven Against Thebes* and
Euripides' *Suppliant Women* and *Phoenician Women;* we might add
Aeschylus' *Persians,* and several plays now lost, including Phrynichus'
historical *Capture of Miletus* (produced shortly after the Persian
capture of the Athenian colony Miletus in 494) and *Phoenician
Women* (date uncertain, but possibly part of the winning tetralogy of

476) as well as various Aeschylean plays which focus on the Trojan War. This pattern is simple in content – recounting a direct conflict between two armies – but it is complex in its dramaturgy, given the impracticability of putting battles onstage. There is accordingly a reliance on narrative strategy, which, in combination with the subject matter, gives these plays a distinctly Iliadic flavour. What is more, the action of such plays must be situated in one city, while the other side is represented through the partisan filter of an envoy or a witness. What is enacted onstage focuses on one side's emotional state and/or practical preparations for the battle. At the heart of the sequence are narrative reports of the battle itself, followed by an exploration of the consequences for both sides, including celebration of victory and lamentation for the dead.

For our play this sequence is initiated at the end of the first episode, overlapping with the resolution of the suppliant pattern, through the Argive Herald's formal threats (275–83), the chorus' uneasiness (288–91) and Demophon's first counter-measures (335–40). The second phase is Demophon's return (389–405) with a military report on both the enemy's progress and his own preparations including divination. In the next scene we receive a general update from Hyllus' Herald (389–401) followed by the specific focus on Iolaus' personal preparations for battle, which resonates with (or rather, jars against) tragic and especially epic precedents.[25] The sequence culminates in the account of the battle delivered by an anonymous slave in a typical 'messenger scene', introduced by a brief stichomythic exchange with Alcmene (799–866).

The sequence appears to be central; not only does it occupy all the episodes of the play between the prologue and the exodos, but it flows smoothly from the initial suppliant sequence and into the final revenge. It would certainly be possible to think of the battle as the central concern of the play. Yet there are two significant disruptions to the sequence that make it difficult to sustain this interpretation. The second of these is the tone of Iolaus' cancelled arming scene in the third episode, as discussed above (pp. 22–3). By undermining the seriousness of these preparations, Euripides also undermines the weight of the larger battle sequence. But the first disruption is the insertion of a separate and distinct pattern in the second episode; the battle sequence is interrupted by the sacrifice of the Daughter. This is related to the battle, but at the same time it remains discrete; the introduction of the new particular crisis, the new focal character and the new resolution distract us from the wider military context. The Daughter refers to the impending battle and the consequences of defeat in her long speech (500–34), but for the rest of this scene there is no mention of either Argos or Athens; the scene's focus is on the Daughter and her focus is on her brothers, herself and her father. Like Iolaus, we lose sight of the battle while caught up in the pathos of the sacrifice scene.

The sacrifice pattern is well calculated to achieve this shift of focus; it is an excruciating dramatic situation, in which a character is ritually killed to satisfy a supernatural power and so to benefit another person or community. Striking variations are possible in the relationships between the cast – victim, killer, beneficiaries and gods – and the overall effect depends significantly on the resistance or compliance of both the victim and the killer. The poet may focus on the decisions leading up to the death, on the description of the offstage sacrifice itself, on the consequences of the sacrifice – all rich dramatic situations. It is a popular sequence in later Euripides (e.g. the deaths of Polyxena in *Hecuba*, Menoeceus in *Phoenician Women*, the title character of *Iphigenia at Aulis,* and Erechtheus' daughter(s) in the fragmentary *Erechtheus*), and it is prefigured in the lengthy account of Iphigenia's death in Aeschylus' *Agamemnon*. It almost certainly featured in several plays now lost and of uncertain date but based on myths which feature sacrifice, including an *Iphigenia* by Aeschylus, an *Iphigenia* and a *Polyxena* by Sophocles, and several Euripidean plays about Phrixus. We might also consider how other deaths, such as the voluntary death of Euripides' Alcestis and the suicide of Sophocles' Ajax, as well as near-deaths, such as the exposure of Euripides' Andromeda and the averted sacrifices of his *Iphigenia at Tauris*, engage with similar concerns about divine causality, the victim and the agent, and benefit to individuals and communities.

In *Children of Heracles* this rich motif is presented very simply. Euripides focuses almost exclusively on the Daughter, with Iolaus and Demophon playing supporting roles in establishing the scenario and providing the expected response. By making the victim not only willing but eager to perform this role, Euripides bypasses most of the moral issues implicit in sacrifice; the nature of the victim eclipses all other considerations. This ethical simplicity is matched by the plot structure; the sacrifice motif is strictly confined to a single episode and ode. The sacrificial character herself is created only for this one scene, and there is no premonition of the sacrifice before this scene and only a single muted mention of it afterward (634). Such constriction of the pattern is unique; in other plays the impact of the sacrifice is expanded through a description of the moment of the sacrifice and its aftermath, and the display and mourning of the body – that is to say, by exploring the response of the survivors. The compression of our play omits this and intensifies the focus of the sequence on the Daughter herself. However, the focus shifts again as the next scene begins; we are encouraged to follow Iolaus' lead and to allow our attention to be captured by the arrival of Hyllus' Herald as the interrupted battle sequence resumes.

The final pattern is perhaps the most familiar tragic plot element to modern audiences: the revenge. The basic sequence, in which an injured party attempts to inflict reciprocal harm on the agent of that injury, occurs throughout mythology and plays from the *Oresteia* to *Bacchae*. Its attraction for the tragedians is obvious: the extremity of the action and of the emotions evoked by it provides rich raw material, while the complexity of sympathies as victim and aggressor exchange roles allows for great sophistication. The nature of the injury – direct or indirect, perceived or real, physical or mental – is easily variable, and tensions can be magnified by a closer relationship between the two parties. The pattern is strongly associated with a contrast if not an outright conflict between private and personal agency against a framework of communal and civic structure. In most revenge tragedies the consequences and cost of the revenge are extensively and climactically explored.

In our play, the revenge is confined to the last scene and most elements of the pattern are again left simple; again the intensity comes from the compression rather than the complexity of the situation. Alcmene is avenging the indisputable injuries inflicted by Eurystheus on her son, herself and her grandchildren. Their kinship, while acknowledged, is not presented as close enough to create any moral dilemma about the appropriateness of Alcmene as the agent of revenge. The focus is instead almost entirely on the problem of how Alcmene can execute her revenge in the context of a civic structure that forbids it, and this problem is resolved abruptly and without any indication of the shape of things to come. We might compare the ending of Sophocles' *Electra* when Orestes brings his father's killer Aegisthus into the house to kill him there, and the play ends. Both playwrights withhold both the actual execution and the consequences of revenge, leaving us no explicit guidance even as to what questions remain unanswered. Are we to adopt the chorus' complacency? To consider the consequences of this action for the city's laws? The moral state of the avenger? To speculate about what might happen next? All of these possible problems and more are left open as the pattern of the revenge stops short. This kind of open ending is common in Greek tragedy, although without knowing more about the sequence of plays it is difficult to assess how striking this effect would be for any particular play.

In *Children of Heracles*, this comes as the last of three abrupt shifts in which a familiar pattern is followed as far as the completion of the focal action but interrupted before the consequences can be explored. This reading emphasizes the immense scope and compression of the play, which are apparent to every audience member, but are particularly intense for those familiar with tragedy who recognize a quick succession of distinct but unresolved patterns.

For some audience members, there may be a further unifying factor in these shifting patterns. Marshall (1998: 84) suggests that the different elements of the play resonate with various facets of Heracles' own persona:

> Euripides ensures that the personality of Heracles imbues each episode with an aspect of his 'mythic history'. Here are five examples: (i) the suppliant drama that opens the play recalls Heracles' own suppliancy in Athens with Theseus; (ii) [the Daughter] Macaria's self-sacrifice mirrors Heracles' own self-sacrificial labours for humanity; (iii) the comic arming scene of Iolaus recalls Heracles the buffoon, so familiar to Athenian audiences from comedy and satyr play; (iv) the battle narrative recalls the archaic development of Heracles as a hoplite; (v) the appearance of Eurystheus who will become integrated as an enemy hero of Athens accentuates the paradox of Heracles, who is the savage civilizer, the uncultured culture hero, and the murderous father.

This is an elegant way of framing the diversity of the play, seeing each element as a reflection of the nature of a multifaceted hero. As we shall see in the next chapter, Heracles is central to the play despite his absence, and this reading of the plot complements other ways in which he can be seen as its guiding spirit.

All of the readings suggested in this chapter highlight the centrality of change – in fortune, associations, plot direction, tone and focal characters – to the experience of the play. But the play does not veer at random; Euripides controls and directs these changes to produce a wonderfully complex and wide-ranging play that accommodates a variety of focus points.

Heracles and Other Imagined Figures

Children of Heracles has no central character. There are many forceful characters and memorable moments, but no single figure commands our attention throughout. Just as each scene presents a new plot twist, each also introduces a new character who initiates the twist and holds the spotlight for a while: Iolaus and the Argive Herald in the prologue; Demophon in the first episode; the Daughter in the second; the Herald of Hyllus and then Alcmene in the third; the Heraclid Slave who acts as a messenger in the fourth; Eurystheus in the exodos. Iolaus and Alcmene are complementary figures who between them remain onstage for most of the play and have prominent speaking parts, but it is difficult to describe the play with either of them as the focal character.

The title of the play itself suggests a broader collective focus, and there are good reasons to consider the interests of the Heraclids as a whole, as we did in the first framework outlined in Chapter 2 (pp. 19–24 above). Euripides presents not the story of a specific child of Heracles – Hyllus or the Daughter – but of his family. The silent group of his children is central to this, and to other aspects of the play as a whole. Marshall, arguing that these children 'function in some sense as character, theme, audience, and stage' (1998: 80–1), draws particular attention to the potentially spectacular effects that a director can create using a large group of children. Yet this group is undeniably passively rather than actively central. There are a few plays, such as Aeschylus' *Suppliant Women* and *Eumenides*, where the chorus that gives its name to the title also dominates the action. This is not the case for *Children of Heracles*. The children do not form the main chorus, and they remain silent and reactive, without the moral agency that we associate with tragic characters. In interpreting the play a collective focus on the Heraclids must be broadened to include Iolaus and Alcmene.[1]

The English translation of the title suggests another way to frame the play's focus: by concentrating on the possessive phrase 'of Heracles'.[2] The stage is largely populated by figures defined both in broader mythology and specifically in the play by their relationship to the absent hero: the young children of Heracles, his companion Iolaus, his mother Alcmene, his Daughter, and his enemy Eurystheus. Through these characters and the doubling and mirroring of their roles[3] Euripides constantly evokes the figure of Heracles for the audience, providing a constant and imposing background that defines and unites the shifting characters in the foreground.

Heracles is not the only important absent figure in the play. Euripides also constructs but does not stage two other mythological figures closely connected to Heracles: his friend Theseus and the eldest Heraclid son, Hyllus. In a curious way, we may say the same of his persecutor Eurystheus; this character does appear onstage, but as a sharp contrast to the image of him that has been constructed in his absence. By keeping the most famous heroes offstage Euripides creates space for others to take centre stage; nevertheless, throughout the play the importance of these absent heroes is strongly felt.

How is this accomplished? The theatre is fundamentally a place of seeing; the process emphasizes showing rather than telling. Nevertheless, though the Greek stage is essentially limited to a specific time and place, tragedy has recourse to many strategies to transcend these boundaries. Offstage events – past and present, as well as predictions of the future – are often recounted during the course of a play, and considerable work has been done in the analysis of this process, with particular attention paid to the 'messenger speech' and the inherent complexity of perspective in drama given the absence of an external narrator.[4] A closely related but more complex phenomenon is the representation of offstage characters – dead and alive, divine and human. Narration and description by other characters are the basis of this process, but the filter of the speaker's perspective is even more powerful in describing an absent character than it is in describing an event; in most cases such speeches give us more information about interpersonal dynamics than about the absent character.[5] An equally important part is played by onstage figures who act as representatives, officially or unofficially, of characters who remain offstage. Furthermore, offstage people may not stay offstage; many plays exploit the dramatic effect of an entrance delayed until the exodos. Even the dead can appear as ghosts (e.g. Darius in Aeschylus' *Persians*) or as *deus ex machina* figures (e.g. Heracles in Sophocles' *Philoctetes*).

Children of Heracles explores a range of ways in which the techniques of constructing offstage characters can be used to generate meaning. Each of the absent figures discussed in this chapter is constructed in a slightly different way and plays a substantially different part in the shape of the play as a whole.

Heracles

Heracles is the most famous of the Greek heroes in modern times as in the ancient world; most of the characters in our play have little independent mythological significance, but are known largely by their connection with him. Accordingly, throughout the play he is the figure by whom almost everyone else is defined, and the initial critical situation – Eurystheus' persecution of the Heraclids – is precipitated by Heracles' relationships with those characters. The play focuses on his offspring whose collective identity depends on their father, who are identified through his name (e.g. 93, 123), and who are imperilled when he dies (e.g. 12–13, 29–30). Iolaus introduces himself to the audience as 'the one man who, honouring the bond of kinship, [...] shared Heracles' many labours' (6–8) and to the chorus as 'Heracles' comrade, Iolaus' (88–9); the chorus later introduces him to Demophon as 'their father's trusted companion, Iolaus' (125). Eurystheus' Herald is identified on arrival as the one who had relayed Eurystheus' commands to Heracles (53–4). Alcmene is first described as 'looking after her son's daughters' (41) and she first arrives onstage when Iolaus summons the 'mother of a noble son, Alcmene' (642). Even Eurystheus foregrounds both his feud and his kinship with Heracles (986–99) early in his first speech.

These references and others provide the basic outlines of Heracles' famous story – Zeus' seduction of Alcmene in Thebes (210, 717–19), the subsequent enmity of Hera (989–90, 1039–40), the labours performed for Eurystheus who was given the throne of Argos instead of Heracles (7–8, 215–19, 945–53), his death and his eventual elevation to Olympus (9–10, 853–7, 871–2, 910–18).[6] Yet these allusions are brief and there is minimal narrative; Euripides' focus is not primarily on the events of Heracles' life, but on his essential excellence – not on the process by which his reputation was established, but the result. In particular we can trace a consistent engagement with the Greek heroic concern with immortality, and three ways in which the legacy of Heracles transcends death: his fame, his children and his qualified divinity.

Fame (*kleos*) is a central concept in Greek poetry focusing on exceptional legendary and historical individuals. It is a common subject but it is also embedded in the function of poetry; for example, the *Iliad* narrates Achilles' quest for *kleos*, but the *Iliad* itself also plays an active role in the establishment and extension of Achilles' fame for both ancient and modern audiences. In our play Heracles' *kleos* is an accepted fact; his reputation is already firmly established shortly after his death. Perhaps the clearest evidence of this is the fact that when Heracles is mentioned in the play as he often is, it is sometimes by name and often by his relationship to the characters onstage (e.g. father, son), but he is also sometimes described elliptically as 'that man' (*ekeinos*) even when he has not been recently mentioned. In these cases his fame and his importance are so outstanding that his name – so often the focus of *kleos* – is not itself necessary and the mere pronoun suffices.[7] For example, when Iolaus hears the Daughter's offer to sacrifice herself he exclaims that she is 'from no other but *that man*' (540), and Alcmene vows that if she lets an enemy take the children away, she should 'no longer be known as *that man's* mother' (651–2). Heracles pervades the play to such an extent that references of this kind are always unambiguous.

Poetic immortality is reserved for very few, but the concept of living on through one's children is as familiar to moderns as it was to ancients. The collective group at the altar embodies this concept; as Marshall puts it, 'the children are a constant spatial-visual reminder of the temporal-unseen immediacy of their father' (1998: 84). Euripides achieves this not only through their continuous presence onstage while other characters come and go, but also through the Greek idea of *eugeneia*, literally 'noble birth,' though often translated simply as 'nobility.' The chorus' sympathy for the children is predicated on this ('I see now a prime example of noble birth being overcome by chance,' 233–5), but so is the danger in which the children find themselves. Despite their emphasized youth and vulnerability as well as their passivity in the play, the Heraclids pose a threat to Eurystheus because they are their father's children, as Demophon fully understands (466–70):

> The king has marched his army here not in search of you [Iolaus] but wanting to kill these [children]. For noble (*eugeneis*) offshoots are a terror for enemies, as are young men who remember the wrong done to their father. It is necessary that he [Eurystheus] should anticipate all these things.

Eurystheus later confirms this (1000–8),[8] but it is essential that this perspective is first voiced by the sympathetic Demophon; the killing of children who might grow up to be a danger, political or personal, is an act of *Realpolitik* for which there is a haunting mythological precedent in the Greeks' killing of Hector's young son Astyanax after the sack of Troy, and similar explanations, while never portrayed sympathetically, are often given in tragedy.[9] In Eurystheus' speech, his fear of the 'hostile offspring of the enemy lion' (1006) is framed as part of his recognition of Heracles' excellence (997–9). The children are assumed to inherit both their father's nature and his enmities, and the threat posed by this legacy is not mitigated by their current vulnerability and passivity.

But Heracles' children are not represented only by the silent group at the altar. The general assumption of the Heraclids' excellence is particularized in our play through the Daughter, whose scene is replete with references to her *eugeneia* and the nature (*phusis*) that she has unmistakably inherited from her father.[10] The Greek text emphasizes the importance of this relationship in a way that is difficult to convey in idiomatic English. For example, she scorns the possibility of the Heraclids being seen as cowards, 'being the children of that father whose children we are' (*patros d' ekeinou phuntas hou pephukamen*, 509), and imagines the indignity of her suffering at enemy hands 'though I am [the daughter] of a noble father' (*patros ousan eugenous*, 513), relegating that fate to others not as distinguished (*episēmos*) as she is (526–7). Iolaus' first response focuses on the same point: 'My child, your spirit is from nowhere else except from that man (*ex ekeinou*); you are by nature (*pephukas*) the Heraclean seed of that divine spirit (*phrenos*)' (539–41). Her second speech, refusing his suggestion that the sisters should draw lots, he calls 'nobler' (*eugenesteros*) than the first (553).[11] The chorus closes the episode with a stanza that seeks to console Iolaus by praising the Daughter (621–9), including the lines: 'she is worthy of her father, and what has happened here is worthy of her noble birth' (*axia men patros, axia d' eugenias tade gignetai*, 626–7).[12] It is worth noting that the emphasis is on kinship and inherited nature, not on any kind of personal influence; just as the play in general focuses on the result rather than the establishment of Heracles' fame, it emphasizes the nobility of the Daughter as her inherent nature rather than the effect of nurture. Indeed, the Daughter gives credit for the latter to Iolaus rather than Heracles in her final speech, saying: 'we are your children; we were raised by your hands' (578).

Notably, it is the Daughter and not Hyllus or another son who is used to make this point; as we will see below (pp. 52–5), Hyllus is a very minor figure in the play. By choosing to focus a scene on an anonymous daughter rather than a named son, Euripides encourages the audience to attribute her qualities not to any independent heroic excellence but to the legacy of the absent Heracles.[13]

But Heracles is not, like most mortals in Greek mythology, restricted to figurative immortality or even the honours paid to dead heroes; the dominant tradition is that he (or at least some part of him) is transformed into an Olympian god.[14] Iolaus refers to this apotheosis near the beginning of the play (9–10), but it subsequently goes unremarked until the description of Iolaus' miraculous rejuvenation (853–7): 'Now you may hear of something wonderful. For two stars standing above the horses' yoke concealed the chariot in a dark cloud; and the wise men say that they were your son and Hebe.' But even this confirmation of his divine status is curiously hedged. The episode – the pursuit of Eurystheus, Iolaus' prayer and the moment of transformation – is distinctly marked as being hearsay (847–8). The deified status of Heracles is therefore not accorded the eyewitness authority of the rest of the Slave's report, so that his direct intervention in the action of the play is conveyed to us as indirectly as possible. We can see echoes of the same prevarication in the responses of Alcmene and the chorus, even as they embrace the news. Alcmene now accepts her son's immortality as a fact, but makes it equally clear that she did not believe it before (871–2). The chorus celebrates Heracles' ascension to Olympus (910–18), but in doing so explicitly describes the alternative – death – that they reject (912–14). Heracles' literal immortality is therefore established for our play, but curiously distanced as well; despite his accepted intervention in the battle he remains a name rather than a concrete presence. Like Persephone, Hebe and Zeus, Heracles the god remains in the background. He continues to be brought to life more strongly through his legacy of fame and children rather than his own divine actions during the play.

Theseus and Athens

In most other versions of our story, the Athenian ruler who protects the Heraclids is not identified, while in some later accounts[15] it is Theseus himself, the friend and contemporary of Heracles. Euripides situates the play after his death, and gives this role to his sons. He is accordingly projected through Demophon and Acamas much as Heracles is represented by his children.[16] Demophon, like the Heraclids, is described as the son of a great father (*esthlou patros pais*, 115), and when Iolaus opens his speech of thanks with the praise of noble birth (*eugeneia*), stating that it is the finest honour 'to be descended from a brave and noble father' (*patros esthlou kagathou pephukenai*, 298), his words apply equally to the Heraclids and the Theseids. When he later promises that after death he will praise Demophon to Theseus in the underworld (320–8), we understand that the son has successfully lived up to his father. We may even interpret this as a subtle allusion to the report that Odysseus gives in *Odyssey* 11 to the dead Achilles anxious about his son; in that episode Odysseus catches sight of Theseus but does not speak with him (*Od.* 11.650–1).

Theseus himself is rarely mentioned in our play, as we might expect given his sons' supporting role. We get only the barest glimpses of his mythology: his maternal genealogy (207–9); the quest for the girdle of Hippolyta (in this version working together with Heracles and Iolaus) and his rescue from the underworld by Heracles (217–19); and the fact of his death (320–1).[17] But there is reason for us to be sensitive to these few mentions: while Heracles was worshipped throughout Greece, by the fifth century Theseus had become the quintessentially Athenian hero.[18] To a largely Athenian audience watching a performance at Athens, Theseus' association with the city is likely to have produced a broader alertness when he is mentioned.

The absence of Theseus and the presence of his sons can therefore be seen as one way of meeting a particular challenge faced by Athenian tragedians: how to reconcile the present democratic ideology with the heroic aristocratic past in which the plays are set.[19] A certain degree of anachronism is a common solution; for example, the Argive king Pelasgus in Aeschylus' *Suppliant Women*, set almost ten generations before our play, long before the establishment of democracy in Athens, explicitly seeks the approval of the people before accepting a group of refugee women and the risk of war with their persecutors. In our play, Euripides replaces the heroic kingship with a more complex intermediary: an emphatically free city (62, 244, 287) under joint rule chosen by lot (34–6), not officially bound to public consultation but sensitive to public opinion (242–6, 335–7, 415–24), and described by a number of terms ranging from *basileis* ('kings') to *prostatai* – literally 'those who stand in front,' and a term often used to describe the leadership in a democracy. By giving Athenian rule to Theseus' sons, Euripides distances Athens from tyranny (e.g. 423–4) while maintaining a close connection with the heroic past.

The silent Acamas plays an important role in achieving this delicate balance despite his negligible contribution to the action because of his particular significance to fifth-century Athenian democracy. After the tyranny of Hippias was overthrown in 510, the politician Cleisthenes reorganized (or 'reformed') the structure of the city, basing political and administrative constituencies not on the four traditional kin groups which reinforced the aristocratic base of power, but on ten newly devised tribes (*phylai*) based on place of residence, each with a local hero for a patron. Acamas was one of the ten heroes, and accordingly performs a silent and symbolic role that is as important as his brother's active one. When the Theseids acquit themselves well – in Demophon's championing of the Heraclids as well as his treatment of the chorus as equals (e.g. 120–31, 271–3) – we may infer that fifth-century democracy has proved itself an appropriate successor to monarchy.[20]

Hyllus

Hyllus' absence is of a different sort; it is not determined by the selected myth, nor is it a subtle detail, but an unexpected element contrived by the poet to achieve a particular focus for the play. The reason given in the play for his absence is simple enough: Iolaus' prologue speech explains that Hyllus has gone with some of his brothers to find an alternate refuge if the appeal to Athens fails (45–7). Having noted and explained his absence, Euripides excludes him from the first half of the play; while Heracles' absence is conspicuous, Hyllus' is discreet. Hyllus is not even mentioned during the two most direct threats to the Heraclids, leaving the most vulnerable members of his family to face the encounter with the Argive Herald and Persephone's demand for a sacrifice. His very errand becomes quietly redundant after Demophon agrees to protect the Heraclids. His complete absence is key to the visual and verbal emphasis on the vulnerability of the Heraclids, their need to find a protector, and their moral stature.

Accordingly, when a Herald arrives from Hyllus (639) the audience needs to be reminded of the master as much as Iolaus and Alcmene need to be reminded of the Herald (638, 658). This unobtrusiveness facilitates a shift in the reason for or at least the result of his absence; there is no mention now of Hyllus' original intentions – to find refuge – but a declaration that he has brought an army (664) of significant size (668–9). The report, delivered as a few lines of pragmatic question-and-answer rather than a continuous narrative description, gives only the roughest sketch of this, focusing on the results rather than the process; we learn nothing of who these allies are or how Hyllus persuaded them to join him. Euripides obscures these details by emphasizing the imminence of battle over other considerations; as a result this report brings Hyllus to the audience's attention without giving a specific impression of him. He recedes further into the background as Iolaus' unexpected determination to join the battle claims our full attention.

Hyllus makes a more significant impact in the account of the battle itself, which opens with his challenging Eurystheus to single combat and a description of the army's approval of the challenge for the consideration and bravery it demonstrates (800–17). This means of distilling and resolving a large-scale conflict is familiar from Homer (e.g. the battle between Paris and Menelaus in *Iliad* 3 and of Hector and Ajax in *Iliad* 7), but also looms large in Hyllus' broader mythology. As briefly mentioned in Chapter 1 (p. 3 above), one of the most well-known episodes of Heraclid mythology is Hyllus' death in single combat against the king of the Tegeans, resulting in the failure of the Heraclids' first attempt to return to the Peloponnese after the death of Eurystheus. For some of the audience, the appreciation of Hyllus' first real focal action must be coloured by this unsettling parallel.[21]

The battle itself ignores not only Hyllus, who steps quietly back into the ranks when his challenge is declined (818), but every other individual. The two generals exhort their troops but no one is singled out in the action; the focus is firmly on the armies themselves until victory is reached at last (842). Only then do individuals re-emerge into the narrative, and Hyllus' part is brief; as he sets out after Eurystheus he is stopped by Iolaus who quickly overshadows him, joining him in his chariot and taking over the reins (843–7), undergoing a miraculous rejuvenation through prayer (848–58), and effecting the actual capture of the enemy (859–66). Hyllus is relegated once again to the edges of our awareness.

Nevertheless, his arrival onstage remains a strong possibility; we may compare the arrivals, effectively deferred until the exodos, of e.g. Aegisthus in *Agamemnon* and Xerxes in *Persians*, as well as later examples such as Heracles in *Trachiniae*. But the arrival of his Herald with the captive Eurystheus dispels this possibility, as we learn that Hyllus and Iolaus are setting up a victory statue to Zeus (936–9). This explanation for his absence is similar in kind to the reason given for his initial absence – a sensible, blameless course of offstage action that produces no immediate impact on the stage action. After this Hyllus is mentioned only once and briefly, when Alcmene asks incredulously whether he agreed to spare Eurystheus' life (967). The Herald answers tartly: 'I suppose he should have disobeyed the land' (968). The indirectness of this reply is astonishingly effective; we understand the state of affairs – Hyllus has not opposed the Athenian decision – but Euripides carefully avoids giving us any description that might have characterized the absent Hyllus, who is otherwise omitted from the final reckoning. He is therefore both accounted for and discounted in the final scene.

Hyllus' absence is made carefully plausible and unremarkable throughout *Children of Heracles*. Yet this absence is one of the most striking and consequential choices made by Euripides in constructing this play. The presence of Hyllus – the son of Heracles, a young man of fighting age – would undercut the initial helplessness of the Heraclids and their aged guardians, and would disrupt the power dynamics in the final scene. By keeping Hyllus absent, Euripides can allow the stage to be dominated by the uneven conflict between Iolaus and the Argive Herald or the uncompromising independence of Alcmene without presenting a weak Heraclid son. The forgettability of Hyllus is one of the subtle masterpieces of this play.

Eurystheus the persecutor

The inclusion of Eurystheus in this chapter might seem counterintuitive, since the character certainly does appear onstage. However, one of Euripides' most effective strategies in this play is to set up a clear expectation of a Eurystheus who does not in fact appear: a relentless and vigorous persecutor who acts as a simple straw man antagonist. He is the most detailed offstage character constructed in this play, and it is instructive to consider how this expectation is built up, and how it is exploded by the arrival of a more nuanced onstage character.

There are several sources for our construction of the absent Eurystheus before he appears in the exodos: the impression given early in the play by his official representative, and descriptions of Eurystheus' character and actions, largely from the Heraclid perspective. Both of these align with the traditional portrayal of Eurystheus in earlier literary and artistic sources as a usurper (e.g. *Iliad* 19.95–125) and a private coward despite his public power, who orders Heracles to perform labours but hides in a jar when confronted with the results (see Fig. 5).

Our early impression of Eurystheus is formed largely from the actions and speech of his herald, on the understanding that he is acting as his master's dramatic representative to the external audience as well as his official representative to the internal audience of Demophon and the Heraclids. This Herald is unambiguously hubristic in every sense of the word: insolent, impious, violent,[22] and boastful. He speaks of the Heraclids almost as if they were escaped slaves, speaking of their 'masters' and 'rulers' (99–100), calling them 'runaways

Fig. 5 A typical depiction of Eurystheus and Heracles. Attic amphora, mid-sixth *c.* BCE. London, British Museum.

from my land' (140) and 'belonging to Eurystheus' (68, cf. 105), and even referring to them as his own property (174, cf. 267). He is ready to violate the sanctity of the altar by striking the old man Iolaus (64–72). He is not bothered by the shamefulness (*aischron*, 255) of his actions, but relies on his status to protect him even as he approaches the altar a second time, explicitly 'testing' the extent of Demophon's resolve (267–73). As Demophon comments, he looks like a Greek, but does not behave like one (130–1). Eurystheus' first representation onstage is unambiguously negative.

Supplementing this initial impression are the many brief descriptions of Eurystheus and his actions throughout the play. The Heraclid perspective of most of the speakers ensures a predictable bias, centring on Eurystheus' *hubris* despite his inferior qualities. This language is introduced early on, as Iolaus recounts Eurystheus' persecution of the Heraclids (*hubrism' es hēmas ēxiōsen hubrisai*, 18). Iolaus later describes him as proud (literally 'thinking no small thoughts', 386) and expects that he will be keen to outrage (*kathubrisai*) an old enemy (456–7), and it is in similar terms that the chorus and Hyllus' Herald characterize his attack on Athens (924–5, 932–4), and Alcmene the labours he laid on Heracles (947, 948). The chorus calls him a fool (360–1, 372), and Iolaus pointedly regrets having such a stupid and unthinking enemy (458–9). Iolaus also considers him too cowardly (*kakos*, 744) to fight, while the Slave describes him as very cowardly (*kakistos*) and unashamed of his cowardice (*deilia*) (813–7).

But equally important is the impression of Eurystheus' military power; after all, Euripides must present his persecution as a real threat to both the Heraclids and Athens for the dramatic situation to have any meaning. The strength of the Argive army is closely associated with Eurystheus' own power; for example, the Herald explains that Demophon could win for Athens 'the great might of Argos and the whole strength of Eurystheus' (156). Similarly, his parting speech (274–83) promises his return with ten thousand troops and 'Lord Eurystheus himself acting as their general (*stratēgōn*)' (277–8), who is waiting nearby and 'will appear vigorous before you and your citizens and your land and its crops' (280–1). He is called a general (*stratēgos*) throughout the play by a range of characters (e.g. 385, 675, 804, 814), and the chorus calls him a lover of war (377–8) and the leader of the Argive army (773–5). Demophon imagines 'Lord Eurystheus' (389) devising his strategy, sitting on a nearby hill considering how to bring his army safely into Attica (393–7), and Iolaus and Hyllus' Herald together imagine him organizing the troops (676–7).

At the same time, his military power must be reconciled with his personal cowardice, and this balance is achieved in part by emphasizing his good luck. Just before he joins the battle, Iolaus explicitly comments that prosperity (*olbos*) is often but wrongly accompanied by a 'reputation for courage,' and that the lucky man (*ton eutuchounta*) is wrongly believed to have exceptional ability (745–7). Eurystheus' power is described in these terms throughout the play, from Iolaus' first report of Eurystheus' threats to the other Greek cities ('saying that it was no small matter to make Argos a friend or a foe, and that he himself was lucky (*eutuchount'*),' 21–2), to his anxiety while awaiting the arrival of 'the general who has been lucky (*eutuchēs*) before' (385), to the Slave's description of 'the general who used to be lucky (*olbion*)' (862–3).

The offstage Eurystheus, accordingly, is a hubristic and unworthy but dangerous general. But when he is brought onstage at 928 this proves to be a caricature rather than a portrait.[23] To some extent this shift is a natural consequence of the change in circumstances. For all practical purposes Eurystheus is no longer a general and certainly no longer a lucky one, and is not in a position that encourages *hubris*. He is not only powerless, but that quintessentially tragic figure – a once-powerful figure who has suffered reversal, and this familiar language is used as he is introduced onstage by Hyllus' Herald (828–40).

His reversal in fortune is matched by the reversal of our expectations; his first words explicitly refute the expectation of his cowardice (*deilia*, 983–5), and both of his speeches begin and end with a calm acceptance of death. The effect of this acceptance is achieved in part by Euripides' suppression of the details of the alternatives. Historically most captives who were not killed were enslaved, a fate often presented in literature as worse than death.[24] But in our play Eurystheus' possible futures are framed simply as death or life. We may contrast this with the Daughter's consideration (and rejection) of several possible future scenarios if she lives (511–27). In Eurystheus' case, we are not invited to consider whether slavery is preferable to death; even when Alcmene tells him that he should count it a benefit to die, it is contrasted not with the real alternative of a wretched life but with the impossible alternative of dying many times over (958–60). As a result, we are presented with a simple valuation of life as unambiguously preferable to death, and his refusal to plead for his life is presented as courage.

Eurystheus now explicitly frames his persecution of the Heraclids not as a personal outrage but as common sense (1000–8), and he implicitly counters the accusation of *hubris* by freely acknowledging Heracles' excellence (997–9) and reminding us that far from being impious he is the protégé of Hera (989–90, 1039–40). The carefully constructed image of Eurystheus is dispelled by the actual character. By creating a traditionally odious offstage character and then dismissing him as a phantom, Euripides first reinforces and then defies the audience's expectations, enabling the extraordinary reversals of the final scene.

4

The Power of the Weak

In the absence of the conventionally powerful, the spotlight falls on the conventionally peripheral. The cast of characters in our play is striking in both its collective social vulnerability and its dramatic marginality. Through the first lens we see a group of young refugee children; an old man, an old woman and an old chorus; a herald alone in enemy territory; a young woman; a slave who covets freedom; a defeated and captive king. Through the second we see a silent group, a silent king and a chorus with a minimal choral role, surrounding a cast of speaking characters of whom half are anonymous, and the other half are second-string mythological figures of limited local importance.[1] Only Demophon – a named, speaking king in his prime – is conventionally powerful and he appears in only two scenes, remaining dramatically secondary to Iolaus in the first and to the Daughter in the second. He is also mythologically minor. There are few stories associated with either Acamas or Demophon, and the two are peculiarly interchangeable, as Kron (1981) demonstrates; the primary distinction between them is that Acamas was an important Athenian hero (see pp. 51–2 above) and Demophon was not. By bringing Demophon forward as the speaking character, Euripides restricts the more significant figure to the background, reinforcing the diffusion of power.

One result of this is the increased importance of representatives and reporting figures. We have already seen the crucial role played by Eurystheus' and Hyllus' Heralds in establishing our impression of their offstage masters. We may add to these the anonymous Slave whose function centres on the delivery of information. 'Messenger speeches' like his account of the battle are a characteristic feature of Euripidean tragedy, and it is now recognized that these speeches are virtuoso performances showcasing the talents of star actors.[2] What is perhaps less obvious is that these three figures shape the course of our whole play; these three anonymous characters[3] appear in and determine the direction of five of the play's six scenes. Only the sacrifice scene does not include such a figure. This is probably incidental rather than deliberate – the result of the absence of Hyllus and the long-delayed appearance of Eurystheus, combined with the demands of the battle sequence – but it is a striking example of the prominence of typically marginal figures in this play.

In focusing on figures characterized by different forms of dependence, Euripides not only draws our attention to unexpected places, but explores more unconventional forms of power as many of the apparently powerless figures in our play contrive to change the dynamics of onstage interaction. It is impossible to give more than a thumbnail sketch of the social and cultural structures that inform these interactions, but each section below addresses a type of conventional powerlessness, outlining the Athenian context as well as the play's particular examples, and considering how that powerlessness may be used, overcome or transfigured.

We will examine first three types of acutely vulnerable figure whose safety depends on a broadly recognized but fragile convention. The importance of such conventions is reflected in the Greek term used; both written laws and unwritten customs are called *nomoi*. The closeness of these concepts is explicitly stated for our place and time period by Thucydides' Pericles, who states that 'in public matters we [Athenians] do not transgress because of our fear, and we are always obedient to those in power and to the laws (*nomoi*), and principally to such laws as are laid down for protection against injury, and the unwritten laws (*agraphoi nomoi*) which it is an acknowledged disgrace to break' (Thuc. 2.37.3). These *nomoi* provide important large-scale protections and reflect cultural and religious values. However, in practice they – particularly the unwritten customs – provide little concrete help in the face of an individual who is willing to accept shame or pollution as a long-term consequence. In our play Euripides tests the limits of the protection provided by such *nomoi*, and the characters' responses to those who threaten to violate them.[4]

Refugees and suppliants

The refugee (*fugas*[5]) is a familiar figure in mythology and in the broader Greek world. It was, as it is now, a desperate plight; refugees had no access to income, and were wholly dependent on the generosity of whatever contacts they possessed. For this reason a refugee is often also a suppliant (*hiketēs*[6]), seeking asylum from a city or petitioning a personal or family connection abroad. Supplication is a powerful social and religious ritual by which a weaker party attempts to place an obligation on a stronger party.[7] In tragedy the suppliant often takes refuge at a public altar or a tomb where he or she may expect divine protection from an immediate threat while awaiting the opportunity to approach a potential human protector. In doing so, a suppliant may add to the general protection of Zeus (under the epithet *Hikesios*) the protection of a specific god. It is important to note that there is not always a clear distinction between the city and the god being supplicated; in our play Iolaus connects the two as he explains 'we have come to Marathon and its neighbouring land and we sit at the altar as suppliants of the gods, [asking] for help' (33–4). Similarly, he describes the Herald's assault upon them as 'a reproach to the city and dishonour to the gods' (71). The fact that they supplicate at the altar of Zeus Agoraios – Zeus of the public marketplace – also implies this connection between the divine and the business of the city.[8]

The physical contact with the altar, where sacrificial fire was lit, is symbolically powerful (though not essential to the supplication).

The altar is normally a sacrosanct space not to be touched by ordinary people, but the suppliant, marked by olive or laurel branches (sometimes wrapped in wool) and wreaths on the head, partakes of a special privilege by contact with this place. Anyone using violence against a suppliant at an altar incurs serious pollution (*miasma*).[9] The most famous Athenian example comes from the seventh century BCE, when the followers of the failed revolutionary Cylon took refuge at an altar but were nevertheless killed by the ruling Athenians, led by Megacles.[10] In consequence Megacles and his family (the Alcmaeonids) were exiled; in some accounts even the bodies of his kin were dug up and removed from the city. His descendants were eventually readmitted to Athens, but the reputation for pollution dogged them into the fifth century. In addition to the pollution brought on those who violate the rights of suppliants, unsanctioned death at the altar and perhaps lesser forms of violence bring pollution to the city itself.[11] The suppliant is therefore protected by both the aggressor's and the city's fear of pollution, and in other plays (e.g. *Helen, Ion*) this proves to be effective. Accordingly, Iolaus in our play tells Eurystheus' Herald that the altar of the god will protect him (61).

Nevertheless, the practical limitation of this protection is immediately exposed by the forceful violation of the altar by the Herald. Such disregard for the conventional sanctity of the altar is a common theme in mythology. For example, when Priam is killed at the altar and Cassandra is raped at the temple of Athena, the transgressors are eventually punished, but their desecrations are not prevented. In tragedy Aeschylus' *Suppliant Women* features an Egyptian herald who prefigures the actions of Eurystheus' Herald in our play in attempting to seize the suppliants from the altar. Euripides will later test the limits of such impious behaviour. For example, in his *Andromache*, Menelaus tricks Andromache into leaving the altar, and when threatened with divine retribution replies 'I'll endure it if and when it comes' (380–440); and again in his *Heracles*, the tyrant Lycus 'persuades' suppliants to leave an altar by threatening to set it on fire (238–51). In these cases the violator is definitely in the wrong.[12] Removing suppliants from a shrine by force is a dishonour to the gods, as emphasized in our play throughout these early scenes (e.g. 70–2, 97–8, 101–4, 107–8, 112–13, 238–9, 258, 260, 264), but there is no expectation that divine retribution for such violation will be immediate. The suppliant is protected by the fear of divine pollution or retribution, but this offers no defence against an aggressor who does not feel that fear. Eurystheus' Herald violates the *nomos* that protects suppliants at the altar, perhaps grabbing a child (65) and certainly knocking Iolaus to the ground (67). But while Iolaus draws attention to the pollution of the suppliants' garlands and the dishonour done to the gods it is to the people of the city that he addresses his cry for immediate help (69–72), and it is the chorus who intervenes and saves the Heraclids.

Even when the Herald's assault is checked, the suppliants remain in danger of rejection. Supplication is often portrayed in literary and visual art as a powerful action and in some contexts seems to amount almost to compulsion; however, it can fail in a number of ways.[13] Even in our play the Heraclids have come to Marathon only after they have been turned away from every other city where they have supplicated for refuge (193–6). In the broader Greek world the outcome was by no means predictable. In most contexts supplication fails as often as it succeeds, and while in some cases this causes disapproval it generally goes unremarked and there is never a religious consequence. The precariousness of the refugee's position adds to the suppliant's vulnerability, as is highlighted in the advice given to a group of refugee women by their father in Aeschylus' *Suppliant Women* (191–203):

> Come as quickly as you can, and hold reverently in your left hands the white-wreathed suppliant branches, the emblems of Zeus whose concern is due respect. Answer any strangers with words that are respectful, pathetic, and show your great need, as is proper for new arrivals, making it clear that you have not been banished

for bloodshed. First and foremost, speak without boldness and
show gravity in your controlled faces and calm eyes. And be neither
quick nor slow in your speech; the people here are very sensitive.
Remember to give way – you are in need, a foreigner, a refugee
(*fugas*). Bold speech does not suit the weak.

In our play the uncertain outcome of supplication is not expressed
in such explicit terms. Nevertheless, Euripides makes Iolaus' plea
distinctive by combining two familiar dramatic forms of supplication.

The Greek terms for supplication do not distinguish between public
and private appeals, and the same principles underlie both.[14] But on the
stage, group and individual supplications produce very different effects.
Group supplication makes for a large-scale tableau and a spectacular
visual impact; it almost certainly takes place in the circular *orchēstra*,
close to the audience, and there is likely to be some physical distance
between the group (at the altar) and the person being supplicated.
Individual supplication, on the other hand, is intensely focused,
involving unusually close physical contact between actors in which
one literally restricts the movement of another by grasping the knees.
The action stops, and immediate resolution is necessary for the play to
continue. This physical difference is also reflected in the nature of the
arguments used by suppliants. Individual suppliants in tragedy often
draw on a personal shared history with the person being supplicated,
while group suppliants and their advocates tend to base their appeals
on larger concepts such as justice and more distant kinship.

Our play combines a public and a personal supplication, as the
initial group supplication of Iolaus and the Heraclids at the altar of
Zeus is later augmented by Iolaus' supplication of Demophon, marked
by the actions of kneeling and grasping his knees and chin (226–31):

I beg you, by the clasp of my hands and by your beard, do not refuse
to take the children of Heracles into your protection. Become their
kinsman, become their friend, father, brother, master – for any
alternative is better than to fall into the power of the Argives.

We have already seen (p. 26 above) how Demophon's acceptance of this entreaty transforms the status of the suppliants as well as the relationship between Athens and the Heraclids. This is a striking visual moment in the play as well as a crucial one for the plot. It is, however, both simply presented and immediately resolved. The claims of the Heraclids as refugees and suppliants are presented unambiguously, and Euripides creates little suspense concerning Demophon's response (we may contrast the lengthy hesitation of his counterpart Pelasgus at Aeschylus' *Suppliant Women* 342–479). The Herald's first attempt to violate the *nomos* that protects them only enhances the strength of their position in the eyes of both internal and external audience, as does his attempt at persuasion. His second physical aggression, however, introduces new questions, as we shall see.

Heralds

The herald is essential to the fabric of Greek society, facilitating a wide range of public functions in both war and peacetime.[15] Fundamentally, however, a herald abroad is a single, generally unarmed man in enemy territory, and Greek society compensated for this with 'religious protection for an exposed but indispensable social function' (Parker 1983: 188). But the extent of this protection, like the suppliant's, depends on the nature of the people he faces. We may compare the position of Agamemnon's heralds in the *Iliad* who are 'unwilling' and 'afraid' to fetch Briseis from Achilles, and are reassured by him that he does not hold them responsible (*Il.* 1.327–36). Heralds are inviolable by custom, but it is always possible that a sufficiently powerful, unscrupulous or provoked enemy will disregard the convention. As Lateiner puts it, 'heralds are the living embodiment [of common bonds and mutual respect], for their lives depend on the legal fiction that enemies are inviolable if they come as "heralds"' (1977: 102–3).

This 'legal fiction' is supported by religious and political consequences, for which we can consider two fifth-century examples. The first is told by Herodotus, who recounts in his *Histories* (7.133–7), that in 491 BCE the Persian king Darius sent heralds to Greece to demand tokens of submission.[16] At Athens and Sparta these heralds were killed, and as a result Sparta incurred divine displeasure which was mitigated by sending two noble Spartans to offer their lives to the Persian king. (Herodotus claims not to be sure of the consequences for the Athenians.) An example from Euripides' lifetime was the killing of an Athenian herald by the Megarians, which was one of several pretexts for significant economic sanctions placed on their city by Athens in 433/2 BCE. But again, the consequences endured by the cities did not protect these particular heralds; as in the case of suppliants, fear of retribution may protect an individual, but only when that fear is felt.

In our play Euripides presents a second test of the limits of the protection provided by fear, not only by making the object of the protection entirely unsympathetic, but also by putting two conventional claims to protection in conflict with each other.[17] After the Argive Herald's first failure to seize the suppliants by force, and his failure to persuade Demophon to give them up, he chooses a very bold course. Consciously relying on his conventionally protected status as a herald, he attempts once again to violate the conventional protection of suppliants at the altar who in addition have now been accepted by the city (267–74):

Herald:	I'll lead them away just the same, taking what is mine.
Demophon:	Then your return to Argos won't be easy.
Herald:	I'll give it a try now and find out.
Demophon:	Touch them and you'll regret it at once.
Chorus:	By the gods, don't dare to strike a herald.
Demophon:	I will if the herald doesn't learn to be sensible.

Chorus: (*to the Herald*) Be off! (*to Dem.*) And you, my lord,
            don't touch him.
Herald: I'm going. For a single man can't put up much of a
            fight.

The Herald explicitly tests the extent of Demophon's respect for the
nomos concerning suppliants, and while he does not succeed in his
aim, he manages to provoke the Athenian king to the point where he
risks violating the *nomos* concerning heralds. This is particularly
striking because Demophon has just declared – in the context of
protecting the suppliants – that he will not pollute the gods (264).
Once again, it is the chorus that intervenes to protect an important
Greek *nomos*, urgently reminding Demophon 'by the gods' not to
use violence against any herald. The king pauses but does not back
down; he is willing to violate the *nomos* protecting heralds in order
to protect the suppliants. The altercation closes with an explicit
reminder of the inherent vulnerability of 'a single man' in enemy
territory, and Demophon's anger is evident in the imprecation
that opens his parting speech: 'go to hell!' (*phtheirou*, literally 'be
destroyed', 284).

   This is a brief exchange but an important one not only for its
characterization of Demophon and the chorus, but particularly
because of its resonance with the earlier scenario and the groundwork
that it lays for the crucial final scene. Because the Herald's attempted
seizure of the suppliants is unambiguously wrong (and his
characterization so odious), Demophon's anger is understandable -
the very word later used by the chorus to describe Alcmene's anger at
Eurystheus (981) – as an instinctive and impulsive reaction. But this
does not alter the essential impiety of his own intended action, any
more than the Herald's own customary protection gives him the
freedom to violate another customary protection. The chorus' quick
intervention does not give us long to feel anxiety over Demophon's

near-violation of *nomos*, and Euripides quickly changes our focus
with Iolaus' speech of gratitude. Nevertheless, we have been primed
for the moral complexities of the final scene.

The prisoner of war

The third character who has a claim to conventional protection is not
immediately presented in that light; when Eurystheus arrives onstage
we are clearly under the impression that he will die without the benefit
of any *nomos*. This expectation is in keeping with mythological and
tragic revenge patterns, and the Slave's account of the capture implies
that Iolaus is merely delaying Eurystheus' execution to gratify Alcmene
(879–87). Her diatribe when he is in her power seems to confirm this
(941–60).

But suddenly, Euripides introduces a *nomos* stating in formal
language that prisoners who are not killed on the battlefield cannot be
executed after their capture (961–72, repeated at 1009–11). The historical
evidence for such a custom is controversial.[18] For example, a passage
often considered in this context is Thucydides' report of the Plataeans'
entreaty to the Spartans after the surrender of their city in 427 BCE.
They appeal to a similar principle, saying: 'It is the *nomos* of the Greeks
not to kill those who have surrendered and who hold out their hands
[i.e. in supplication]' (Thuc. 3.58.3), and they point out that their deaths
will bring infamy (*duskleia*) and baseness (*kakia*). It is noteworthy that
they explicitly connect their captive status with their voluntary surrender
and supplication – both actions that Eurystheus explicitly rejects
(885–7, 984–6). It is also important that these arguments (and many
others) do not save the Plataeans; the men are killed and the women
sold into slavery. This is not an unusual historical result; accounts from
the Peloponnesian War and other contexts show that prisoners of war
were killed as often as they were spared, and while there are sometimes

moral judgements of these executions there is no evidence that any particular religious pollution was attached to them.[19] Nevertheless, pleas of this kind suggest that the idea of captives' sanctity is likely to have resonated with a fifth-century audience at least in theory.

The ambiguity of the authority of this *nomos* is an integral element in the final scene. It is perfectly reasonable for the protection of captives to be accepted in the world of the play as an important local Athenian *nomos*, especially as it is first put forward by a third party (Hyllus' Herald) with no direct investment in the result. When it is mentioned again it gains a more powerful dimension – though this time we have only Eurystheus' word for it – as a generalized Greek custom with divine as well as human sanction (1011–13), putting it on a par with the protection of suppliants and the immunity of heralds. Crucially, however, Alcmene is not aware of this *nomos* until it is mentioned by Hyllus' Herald (963), and it is perfectly plausible that she does not. Her willingness to violate it is accordingly of a different kind from the Argive Herald's deliberate actions against the suppliants and Demophon's angry movement against the herald; she has no reason to fear the religious consequences of violating a *nomos* that she does not know. In the absence of this fear, only external intervention can protect Eurystheus. The chorus does begin to do so (1018–19), but they are interested only in the letter of the *nomos* (1021) even before they learn of the benefits that Eurysthcus' death will bring. Earlier thcy intervened to protect the suppliants and the herald, but in the end they collude in the execution of the prisoner of war (1055).

We must also note that while Iolaus (speaking for the suppliant Heraclids) and the Argive Herald want to preserve the *nomoi* that protect them, Eurystheus does not. While his first speech proclaims the inviolability of captives and the religious sanctions against killing him now (1011–15)[20] as well as his indifference to his own fate, his second speech encourages Alcmene to violate this *nomos*, opening with an explicit invitation to kill him (1026),[21] while also providing the chorus with an extraordinary incentive to permit this violation. We may compare the way in which his Herald earlier dared Demophon to lay hands on him, but both Eurystheus and Alcmene are far more committed to their course of action. The *nomos* – or more specifically the consequences of its violation – becomes a weapon with which Eurystheus, having lost the battle, can posthumously ruin Heracles' family by giving up his life as well.

The power of this weapon and of Eurystheus' death is amplified by the prophecy of Eurystheus' transformation into a cultic hero, a dead man who exerts power in the area near his grave and receives certain honours. As a result, the consequences for violating the *nomos* go beyond general divine displeasure and pollution, compounded by the enmity of his specific heroic power.[22] Now, it is not uncommon in Euripidean tragedy for cult honours to be established for a dying or dead character, sanctioned by divine authority within the play and usually connected with a historical cult in the real world.[23] In such cases a character who has been in some way victimized is granted a transcendent power and a form of immortality. But Eurystheus is given an unusual degree of agency in this process. In most cases the cult is announced by a *deus ex machina*, but in lieu of a direct divine disclosure Euripides has Eurystheus reveal the prophecy of his own cult.[24] The prophecy accordingly retains a very personal focus on Eurystheus' old enmity with the Heraclids and his new alliance with Athens based on their respect for his status as a prisoner, and as we have seen in Chapter 2 (pp. 30–2 above), Eurystheus' speeches are rooted in the language of hatred rather than attachment. Protecting the future Athens is framed as a means of punishing the Heraclids.

Euripides' introduction of the uncertain tradition regarding captives is a skilful culmination to his sequence of protective *nomoi* and the limitations of their power, creating a further and unexpected reversal of fortune in the final moments of the play. Through the violation of that *nomos* Eurystheus gains a range of victories: by dying he ensures Alcmene's pollution, his personal persecution of Heracles' descendants long into the future, and the division of Heraclid and Athenian interests. It is perhaps not to be wondered at that he is ready to meet his death.

The human sacrifice

Animal sacrifice is recognized as a cornerstone of ancient Greek religion, but our picture of human sacrifice is much less clear.[25] Until recently there has been no archaeological evidence that the Greeks ever performed human sacrifices,[26] and there are relatively few representations of the phenomenon in art;[27] it was certainly not a part of mainstream Greek religion. But it is mentioned by authors from Homer to Pausanias as both a mythological and a historical phenomenon. The majority of these stories are removed in time and place from classical Athens,[28] but it was (like other extreme actions) a rich subject for Athenian tragedians and their audiences. In addition to the plays that feature an explicit human sacrifice, many non-ritual deaths in tragedy are described using the imagery of the perverted sacrifice, including the famous death of Agamemnon in Aeschylus.[29]

In the literary descriptions of human sacrifice that definitely precede our play – in Homer (*Iliad* 23.175–6), Pindar (e.g. *Ol.*1.23–66), and Aeschylus (e.g. *Ag.* 192–251) – the person sacrificed is an innocent and powerless victim, either a passive object with no articulated perspective (like Homer's Trojans or Pindar's Pelops) or an unwilling sufferer (like the gagged and terrified Iphigenia described by Aeschylus). The agency of the sacrifice belongs entirely to the one who chooses to perform the sacrifice. It is in this way that Euripides initially frames the problem of the sacrifice in our play, presenting it to us through the eyes of the king. Demophon reports his dilemma and the choice he has made for himself and on behalf of other fathers: 'I will not kill my own daughter nor will I force another of my citizens against his will. And who is so foolish that he will willingly give away his children?' (411–14). This perspective is taken up by Iolaus at 435–6 as he considers the situation and again at 492–3 as he explains the situation to the Daughter; it is the parent or guardian who is considered as the agent.

The Daughter shifts that perspective, claiming the agency of the sacrifice. This will become a Euripidean motif – the voluntary self-sacrifice – but this may be the earliest example of it.[30] Certainly in no other extant example is this agency seized more strongly than here. In most cases for which we have the relevant information the victim is pre-determined and begins by resisting (although in the case of Menoeceus in Euripides' *Phoenissae* this resistance turns out to be feigned). For chosen victims like Iphigenia and Polyxena only one very limited kind of agency is possible: the agency of acceptance.[31] In our play the Daughter does not merely accept but volunteers,[32] a situation that Euripides makes possible by specifying a type of victim rather than an individual.

Furthermore, the Daughter explicitly refuses the traditional casting of the sacrifice as a victim. When Iolaus suggests that she and her sisters should draw lots to determine who should die, she categorically refuses (539–51); her self-sacrifice is a 'favour' (*charis,* 548) that depends on her complete freedom of choice (551). Accordingly Euripides shows not a shift from a reluctant to a willing victim (as he does in other plays), but from a dependent suppliant to an active saviour.[33] What is more, the Daughter's self-sacrifice is also framed as the fulfilment and proof of her noble nature, a moral complement to the physical perfection required of a sacrifice.[34]

The Daughter's age and virgin status are (by Greek standards) part of this physical perfection. Though Persephone does not name a victim she specifically demands an unmarried girl (*parthenos,* 408). This 'bride of death' archetype will be Euripides' favourite type of character for the self-sacrifice motif, and in many other plays the intersection of marriage and death rituals are highlighted.[35] In our play, however, this particular connection is not emphasized; the Daughter does ask to die in women's hands rather than men's (565–7) and she briefly mentions the marriage and children that she will not have (579, 591–2), but this lost future is a relatively minor consideration. It is also striking that the Daughter offers her life without anyone raising strong objections.[36] With the older of her brothers away and Iolaus left helpless by the disastrous news – that is to say, in the absence of a strong male guardian[37] – there is no other character in a position to dispute her claim to agency in her sacrifice.

This shift from powerless victim to consenting agent seems to reflect earlier developments in the visual portrayal of human sacrifice. Mylonopoulos notes a transition from the earlier archaic focus on the gory sacrifice of a struggling or restrained victim to a fifth-century presentation of a patient and tranquil victim in the moments before the sacrifice itself, while depictions of killing at an altar tend to portray transgressive killings without ritual sanction (2013: 83–4). The idea of the consenting sacrifice is therefore likely to have been familiar to Euripides' audience, even if this is one of the earliest such examples in tragedy. What is striking in our play is more the extent of the Daughter's agency than the fact of her consent.

Children and old men

Childhood and old age are both physically vulnerable states with limited legal rights, religious protection and social power in the Greek world. Their dependent states are closely associated through mythological examples (e.g. Hector's son Astyanax and his parents Priam and Hecuba in representations of the sack of Troy, or Aeneas' son Ascanius and his father Anchises), as well as in proverb: 'old men are children twice.'[38] The tragedians also associate the two vulnerable states; for example, the chorus of old men in Aeschylus' *Agamemnon* explicitly lament their childlike fragility (*Ag.* 75–82), while our own play makes the connection visually and implicitly. Both ages are avoided by the anthropomorphized Olympian gods, who pass quickly from birth to their mature forms and then do not age.

The two states are also linked by their universality. The other categories so far discussed are all extreme or restricted cases, but childhood and old age are directly relatable to every audience member regardless of status, gender and circumstance. A great deal of their dramatic power lies in their familiarity.

Children

Children in Athens, as in many other societies, lived a precarious existence which has been painstakingly traced in recent years despite the fragmentary nature of the evidence.[39] Infants could be left to die at the discretion of the head of the family – usually the father – or sometimes civic authorities. Such exposure carried neither religious stigma nor legal penalties, although there may have been some social repercussions.[40] Literary sources show that children were viewed less romantically than is often the case in the modern Western world; Golden (2015) goes so far as to state that 'children were regarded as physically weak, morally incompetent, mentally incapable,' (4) though 'loved and enjoyed' despite their limitations (9).

Children appear in at least ten of our extant tragedies, but they tend to be either silent or heavily stylized.[41] The age of tragic characters is never specified, as is usually the case in literature based on mythology – and indeed, many people in the ancient world probably did not have a clear idea of when they were born.[42] Nevertheless, we can gather some clues from the demands of the text. It is clear from the staging in some plays, such as Sophocles' *Ajax* and Euripides' *Trojan Women*, that some roles must be played by young children who can be easily lifted by an adult actor. At the same time, these children must both move independently and stand quietly for long periods of time; there is no question of representation by dolls or by very young children. In our play, the Heraclids may have been played by actors in a slightly older age range. They are not physically carried or lifted, and they must all be old enough both to remain onstage for the duration of the entire play – an unusual situation for any character in tragedy – and to perform the choreography of the scene in which they shake hands with the chorus (307–8). Some of them must be big enough to help Iolaus to the altar and cover him when he collapses after the departure of their sister (602–4), but as a group they must be small enough not to contradict the linguistic emphasis on their youth (e.g. 'small,' 24; 'new-raised boys,' 91; 'infants,' 956). In addition, we know that the oldest brothers have accompanied Hyllus on a separate mission (45–6), and Iolaus adopts a protective stance that requires a clear difference in stature (though a sitting posture would help to some extent). When the old man states 'I have taken these children under my wing and protect them' (10–11) or when he instructs them to take hold of his robes as the Argive Herald approaches (48), the pathetic impact depends partly on their size; if all or most of the actors playing the children were close to Iolaus' size the effect would be at least partly ironic.

The children in our play are typical in that they are primarily presented as passive victims, reacting to events around them without taking an active role. They are never individualized by names or speech or description, and they are never given independent agency. They provide a constant visual focal point, frequently pointed to both literally and verbally. They are the conceptual heart of the play as a link between past and future generations; they are initially persecuted as the sons of Eurystheus' enemy, and at the end of the play they are

presented as the forefathers of Athens' enemies. They are objects of
pity and fear, but they are not subjects developed as characters.[43]

Old men

The rise of scholarly interest in ancient childhood has been paralleled
by an interest in old age, for which we have rather more evidence and
considerable variety in interpretation.[44] Brandt (2012) demonstrates
that there is abundant evidence for the appreciation of the elderly and
for their integration – especially the able-bodied and clear-minded –
into the community. We know of some extraordinary creative individuals
who continued to produce great works in their eighties or beyond,
including the poet Simonides and Euripides' contemporary Sophocles.
Athenian citizens were legally obliged to care for their parents
(*gerotrophia*, of which our earliest evidence is fragments 55–7 of Solon's
laws, sixth *c.* BCE), and this is reflected in tragedy when parents who
lose children lament the implications for their own old age (e.g. *Medea*
1029–37, 1395; compare Alcmene's worries in our own play, 712–16).
Nevertheless, there was no centralized provision for the elderly and it is
clear that on the whole the old had little political power.[45]

Old age is frequently discussed in literary sources which reflect the
diversity of individual experience. Nestor in the *Iliad*, whose age
and experience confer a certain status on him (despite the variable
reception and results of his advice), acknowledges but gracefully
accepts the limitations of old age (*Il.* 4.313–25); we can compare
the juxtaposition of the wisdom and powerlessness of the old men
on the walls of Troy (3.146–244). Plato's *Republic* opens with a brief
conversation about the advantages of old age for those in comfortable
circumstances. But many descriptions are intensely negative.[46] For
example, the *Homeric Hymn to Aphrodite* contrasts the glories of
immortality not primarily with death, but with the indignities of old

age: 'pitiless old age, the future that stands beside mortals, hateful, wearying, which even the gods shrink from' (245–6). A similar attitude is reflected in a myth – of which there are no written accounts, but five surviving vase-paintings from the first half of the fifth century – of Heracles fighting Geras, the divine personification of old age,[47] aligning it with the other monsters and ills that plague humanity.

Old men appear frequently in tragedy, both as choruses and individual characters, and they often share the physical weakness of children if not their passivity.[48] They are acutely aware of the youthful power – specifically physical strength and its corresponding influence – they have lost and which they lament. For example, in Euripides' *Heracles* the hero's father Amphitryon and the chorus of old men repeatedly mourn their lost strength, and the chorus wishes earnestly that the gods would let the virtuous be young twice.[49] Old men who manage decisive or forceful action do so in spite of their age; for example, Peleus in *Andromache* arrives declaring 'now it is time for me to recapture the strength of my youth, if ever' (553–4), and refers to his age throughout his successful encounter with a hostile Menelaus.

In our play too the emphasis is almost entirely on the physical vulnerability of age, and Iolaus' old age and its attendant weakness are constantly mentioned throughout his time onstage, pointed out by himself and every other speaking character. Particularly barbed is Eurystheus' Herald's description: 'an old man with one foot in the grave, who is really nothing as the saying goes' (166–7), but almost as deflating is Demophon's refusal of Iolaus' offer of self-sacrifice by pointing out that Eurystheus gains nothing by 'the death of an old man' (466–7). In addition to these verbal markers, Iolaus' physical weakness is driven home by three moments in the staging: first in the exchange with Eurystheus' Herald, when he is knocked to the ground (67–72, 127–9); next when he collapses after the Daughter leaves the stage (602) and is unable to raise himself when Hyllus' Herald first arrives (636); and most pitilessly of all in the central scenes with Hyllus' Herald

(680–747), especially as he moves slowly offstage, leaning on the young man 'like a child' (729) while urging him to go faster.[50]

Iolaus' last speech onstage begins with a wish to regain the strength of his youth, and the miraculous fulfilment of this wish is the play's most explicit empowering of the weak, a true reversal not just of external fortune but of nature. It is also, I suggest, presented as the least important. It is difficult to know whether an external tradition might have suggested this development to an informed audience member,[51] but for many the only clue is his parting prayer. What is more, it is doubly distanced from the audience; not only is it an offstage event, but the reporting Slave has not even witnessed it himself (847–8). Most surprisingly, this miracle draws almost no comment from other characters. When the Slave first reveals it in the preamble to his long narrative, saying 'he has changed back from an old man to a young one!' (796), Alcmene's laconic response (only two words in the Greek) is 'You have told a wondrous tale' – and she then asks not for the details of this miracle, but for a general account of the battle. When the complete tale is told, both the chorus and Alcmene rejoice in the proof of Heracles' divine status, but make no reference at all to Iolaus' rejuvenation. Alcmene asks only – with some acidity – why Iolaus spared Eurystheus (879–80), and the chorus does not mention him at all. When Hyllus' Herald arrives onstage in the exodos, he mentions only that Hyllus and 'good (*esthlos*) Iolaus' are busy offstage (936); this character, whom we last saw in a scene entirely focused on Iolaus' old age, does not not make any reference to his rejuvenation. Nor does Eurystheus mention his captor at all.

We may attribute this at least partially to a shift in focus from Iolaus to Alcmene; however, we may also consider that to Euripides' audience the rejuvenation is in some sense a restoration of the expected – not on the uncertain supposition that some might be familiar with an obscure tradition, but simply because of the usual identification of Iolaus as Heracles' nephew rather than a kinsman from his mother's generation. He is elsewhere in myth consistently presented as a young warrior, and his religious cult was associated with athletic games and in some places with gods such as Hebe (youth) and Kourotrophos (child-nurturer).[52]

Euripides accordingly presents Iolaus' rejuvenation as almost incidental. Like other miraculous offstage events reported in Euripidean tragedy, such as the bull that emerges from the sea to kill Hippolytus or the various wonders described in *Bacchae*, Iolaus' rejuvenation is of passing interest; the focus is on the final consequences of the miracle and the power of the divinity that brings it about. When Iolaus does not return to the stage he ceases to be a focus of attention, and the exaggerated vulnerability of his old age is as much displaced in our interest as it is replaced by his rejuvenated strength.

We may contrast the fixed but understated old age of the chorus.[53] We can reasonably assume that they are marked as old by white hair and beards which certainly would persist throughout the play. However, their age is mentioned only once, as Demophon praises their quick response to the cry for help, 'surpassing younger men' (120). We can only speculate as to whether their movement reflected their age, but there is certainly no verbal indication of physical infirmity; we may contrast the extended emphasis on the age of other choruses of old men.[54] Nor are they socially marginalized; Dhuga draws attention to what he calls 'the politico-ritual authority' of our chorus during the episodes (2011, ch. 2), and connects their 'choral battle-odes' with Nestor's encouragement of his men in *Iliad* 4 (2011: 5). One possible effect of this, in conjunction with the setting of the play at Marathon, is an anachronistic but powerful connection between the chorus and the warriors of Marathon (*Marathonomachoi*) who won a landmark battle against the Persians in 490 BCE.[55] The veterans of that battle were held in high esteem, and there may even have been a few in Euripides' audience.

It is possible that there is one further instance of old age in our play: Eurystheus may be marked as an old man by white hair, though his age is never verbally indicated. He is first cousin (*autanepsios*, 987) to Alcmene just as Theseus and Heracles are the children of first cousins (*autanepsiōn*, 211). Now, there can be significant age gaps between first cousins, and this genealogy is consistent with the Homeric account in which Eurystheus is only a few hours older than Heracles but is also the grandson of Perseus (*Iliad* 19.95–133), while Alcmene is typically the granddaughter of Perseus as she is in our play (210). If Euripides' Eurystheus is, like Homer's, the same age as Heracles and still in his prime (that is to say, if he appears with dark hair), then his vulnerability as a defeated king contrasts most strikingly with Demophon. If, however, he does appear with white hair, then he invites comparison with Iolaus.[56]

What is more, his appearance as an old man would be the first reversal of several in the exodos. In addition to the tensions this would bring to the final scene itself, it would also have a retrospective effect on the account of the battle. The victory of Hyllus and Iolaus as relayed in the Slave's speech owes much of its glorious flavour to the assumption that Eurystheus is a vigorous rival, and therefore a coward for refusing Hyllus' challenge (813–17) and a worthy prize for capture (859–60). This would be undercut if we are suddenly faced with the fact of his age: we would then no longer be presented with the meeting of equals on the battleground, but the pursuit of an old man by the young – closer to Priam and Neoptolemus than Hector and Achilles. This would seriously undercut the Heraclids' moral position even before Alcmene embarks on her vengeance.

Women

Having considered the focus that Euripides brings to different kinds of powerlessness over the course of the play, we now turn to one that is not strongly marked verbally, but which is an integral part of the

Greek world and inherently focal for many audience members. Awareness of gender is built into the language itself and reflected in the world of the play, from the segregation of Heracles' daughters indoors while the sons remain outside (40–4) to Iolaus' rejection of Alcmene's opposition to his intention to fight, saying: 'fighting is men's business; yours is to care for these [children]' (711). In this context, both women in our play display remarkable strength of will, and while both acknowledge the potential for their initiative to be seen as audacity (*thrasos*) inappropriate in a woman, neither allows this consideration to deter her from her course of action.

When the Daughter steps out from the temple uninvited into public space populated so far only by men, she begins with a speech of explanation. In it she specifically anticipates that her appearance could be construed as audacity and requests that it not be taken in this way; she then acknowledges the general precept that 'silence and modesty are most becoming for a woman' and admits that she herself is 'not chosen to represent the family'; nevertheless she meekly claims that she is 'somehow suitable' and has a special concern 'for my brothers and myself' (474–83). One effect of this remarkable defensive speech, disclaiming both boldness of character and authority of status, is to forestall and diffuse anxiety about her initiative in appearing.[57] But having achieved this, the Daughter adopts a fully assertive and authoritative tone, using a mix of imperatives and rhetorical questions to support her statements. She proposes a decisive course of action (500–34), rejecting Iolaus' proposed revision (543–51) and earning the unreserved praise and acquiescence of all her onstage hearers.[58] It is not forgotten that she is a woman (e.g. 523–4, 565–6, 570–1, 591–2), but her gender is not raised by any other character as a potential source of criticism – it is, after all, a female life that Persephone demands. The Daughter raises the matter of her own gender for one critical moment and then it is dropped as a possible criticism of her agency.

Alcmene employs a similar technique – not on the occasion of her first appearance, which is a response to a summons rather than an independent initiative, but when she entrenches herself in her decision to kill Eurystheus, declaring: 'anyone who likes will say, "This woman is bold (*thrasus*) and thinks bigger thoughts than a woman ought to." But this deed will be done, and by me' (978–80). Like the Daughter, she acknowledges the traditional restrictions on women and anticipates the criticism of her audacity; but where the Daughter tactfully disarms this criticism, Alcmene dismisses it.

There is no doubt that the two women in the play are a significant pair; there is parallelism or inversion in almost every aspect of their roles, from their emerging out of the sacred space of the temple to the exceptional agency of their actions, and these may well be emphasized by similarities in their costume and perhaps by the doubling of these roles by the same actor.[59] But for many audience members this is the extent of the play's engagement with gender. The same tactics that work on the internal audience of men onstage also work on these members of the external audience: for them the question is raised but then dropped, and the focus shifts to other aspects of the agents before us.

For others, gender lies at the heart of the whole play. For example, Burnett (1998: 145–57) frames the play as a series of dilemmas in which 'the masculine world is so hampered by its own pompous civility that it cannot rid itself of an egregious evil, and consequently a woman has to do the job' (145). For Mendelsohn, the two women are at the heart of the Euripidean version of the story (2002: 14–18), each placed at the centre of a mythically innovative scene as a crucial engagement with contemporary concern about appropriate male and heroic behaviour within a democratic context. Roselli focuses specifically on the Daughter, and views her gender as 'a disguise for class' (2007: 82), making her a figure with whom both elite and non-elite members of the audience can identify, with implications for the socio-political function of drama. All of these readings have their strengths, but their success depends on a spectator's own sensitivity to and readings of the gender of the characters onstage. Many tragedies from *Agamemnon* to *Bacchae* feature the relations of the sexes and the text explicitly focuses our attention on these elements. This play is not one of those.

In a famous passage, the comedian Aristophanes creates a caricature of Euripides who boasts of his 'democratic' cast of characters, saying that the woman, the slave, the master, the girl and the old woman all speak in his plays (*Frogs* 948–52, produced in 405 BCE). The comic exaggeration of this passage is barely discernible when we consider it in the light of *Children of Heracles*. This play gives not only voice but power to the conventionally powerless.

Then and Now

So far I have concentrated on what might be called the more universal aspects of the play's interpretation – those which depend primarily on the text of the play itself and on broad rather than specific context. We turn now to the importance of narrower context, including two thorny and superficially dissimilar topics: the date and immediate political resonance of the original and later performances, and (briefly) the scholarly reception of the play. I have left these issues to the last because I believe that they have unduly dominated the critical discussion of our play. We cannot date the play (or indeed most ancient plays) precisely, and this limits our ability to discuss the particular contemporary implications meaningfully, quite apart from the broader methodological question of how specifically tragedy ever alludes to contemporary events. As for the treatment of *Children of Heracles* by scholars I particularly regret a damaging tendency, even in those who admire the play, to repeat the history of the play's assessment rather than its interpretation; this is more of a distraction than a help and, I believe, has done more to limit the appreciation of this play than is generally realized. Having considered the play on its own terms it is now time to examine how far our understanding of the play is influenced by these essential ancient and modern contexts.

Dating Euripides

Scholarship abhors a vacuum. There is a strong desire to supply dates, however approximate they must be, in order to provide context, just as there is a desire to name unknown authors and anonymous characters in order to facilitate discussion and reference. Because of their usefulness, dates put forward on shaky grounds often pass into common use with qualifiers such as 'approx.' or at best a range of possibilities to acknowledge the uncertainty of our information. These shorthand qualifiers, however, do not indicate the degree of our uncertainty, and even when a range is given it is unclear whether all dates are equally likely, or whether the middle of the range is to be preferred (as we often assume, as if history were subject to arithmetical averages).

Half of Euripides' plays can be dated from external records preserved in the manuscripts. For the remainder, including *Children of Heracles*, we rely on a method rooted in the remarkable observation of Hermann, who in 1807 noted a consistent pattern in Euripides' use of a particular metrical technique: resolution (the substitution of two short syllables for one long) in iambic trimeter (the metre used for spoken verse in tragedy) occurs more frequently in the five late datable plays compared to the three early ones. Hermann suggested the potential of this feature in deducing the dates of otherwise undated plays.[1] Other scholars have since painstakingly translated this insight into data, counting the occurrences of resolution in Euripides' spoken verse, and have established the general strength but also the particular uncertainties of the pattern observed by Hermann.[2] It is a sound methodology for establishing an approximate chronology, but it is not sufficiently robust to date specific plays with confidence, particularly for the earlier plays. Most importantly for our purposes, it is not until the five later datable plays (the earliest performed in the year 415) that we see a change; the three earliest Euripidean plays, which span from 438 to 428, use more or less the same low (single-digit) rate of resolution, as do all extant plays of Aeschylus and Sophocles. *Children of Heracles* also uses a single-digit resolution rate. Given so few data points, a play with a low resolution rate like ours is statistically equally likely to have been produced as early as 445 or as late as 420.

To supplement the imprecise metrical evidence scholars often seek to map events or references within a play onto particular historical occurrences. The most well-known example of this is Sophoclean rather than Euripidean, but it will serve to demonstrate the process. We have no evidence at all for the date of *Oedipus Tyrannos*. But in 1800[3] Samuel Musgrave proposed that the plague at the beginning of the play should be identified with the disastrous Athenian plagues of 430–426, and that the play can accordingly be dated to shortly thereafter. This proposal was taken up and elaborated by others, including an influential article by Knox (1956) and a recent chapter by Mitchell-Boyask (2008, ch. 5). Some scholars have pointed out the weakness of this proposal; even if we accept that Sophocles is alluding to a specific outbreak of plague (and we have some evidence to suggest that references to disastrous contemporary events were avoided), plagues were a common enough occurrence in the ancient world.[4] In addition, the historical event gives only a *terminus post quem*; the play must be written after the fact, but there is no way of determining how long after. Nevertheless, 429 (suitably qualified) has made its way into most encyclopedia entries, introductions and dustjackets of translations, and even some works of scholarship on *Oedipus*.[5] It seems that we prefer an unconvincing date to no date.

Various dates have been proposed for *Children of Heracles*, but none is conclusive.[6] Nevertheless, *Children of Heracles* is commonly dated to 430 (approx.) because of the explicit foreshadowing of a future invasion of Athenian territory by the descendants of the Heraclids, first alluded to at lines 310–19 and expanded at 1030–44 as Eurystheus reveals that he will become a hero, and will be 'most hostile to the descendants of these [children] when they come here with a powerful army, betraying this obligation (*charis*) [to you]' (1034–6), giving them a 'terrible return-journey' (*kakon noston*, 1042).

The predicted invasion is almost always taken as a reference to the foray into Attica by the Spartans at the end of April 431, which is usually considered as the official beginning of the second (or Archidamian) Peloponnesian War. Because this is framed as part of a specific prophecy, it is more plausible as an allusion to contemporary fifth-century events than circumstances belonging to the in-play chronology like the plague from Sophocles' *Oedipus*. Yet with this kind of reference point we cannot even be sure that the play was performed after the event; tensions between Athens and Sparta had been ongoing for decades. Unlike the plague of 430, which could not possibly have been foreseen by an audience in 431, the Spartan invasion of April 431 was almost certainly anticipated, as we will see shortly. Euripides couches the prophecy in such general terms that it might well have been a forecast for his external audience as well as for Eurystheus' internal one.

What is more, even if we accept that Euripides is referring his audience to a contemporary event, the invasion of 431 is not the only candidate. The year 431 was the beginning of the second and more famous Peloponnesian War, but the first one, which began in 460, also included a Spartan invasion of Attic territory, although Athens itself was not reached. In 446, the Spartan general Pleistoanax led an army as far as Eleusis – only 18 km northwest of Athens. He plundered Eleusis and the surrounding area before abandoning the invasion (Thuc. 1.114, 2.21), and was later exiled for this; our sources suggest that he was either persuaded or perhaps bribed by Pericles to withdraw (Thuc. 2.21, Plutarch *Pericles* 22–3). It is possible that this abandoned invasion of 446 is the one alluded to in *Children of Heracles*, and that the oracle about Eurystheus' heroic protection refers Euripides' audience appreciatively back to a peril successfully avoided rather than optimistically forward to a desired outcome. This would place the play approximately fifteen years earlier than generally believed, but still well within the span of Euripides' productive career (ten years rather than twenty-five after his first competition in 455) and consistent with the metrical evidence.

I do not propose 445 BCE as a probability but as a possibility. There is no more evidence for this date than there is for the conventional one – but neither is there less. Our current information does not allow us to be confident of even the decade of the play's dating. Yet knowing when a play was performed undeniably affects how we understand it, and it is worth exploring some of the potential implications of the different possible dates.

Possible Athenian performance contexts

Children of Heracles was certainly received by some of its original audience as an explicitly political piece. There is no doubt that the Peloponnesian War provided the general background to our play and heightened the original audience's sensitivity to both direct and indirect references to Athens, Sparta and military affairs in general. There is equally no doubt that some elements of the play would have resonated with specific contemporary events. However, since we cannot ascertain the date of performance, we must be sensitive to the immense range of possible allusions offered by the dynamic politico-historical context of the Peloponnesian Wars, and conscious of the speculative nature of any interpretations that depend on a specific year. The difference between 432 and 428 BCE is as significant as the difference between 1912 and 1916 CE; it matters immensely whether it was performed before or after the official outbreak of war. Similarly, the difference between 445 and 430 BCE is as significant as the difference between 1919 and 1946 CE. If we knew the specific date of production, we would undoubtedly be able to make some very constructive connections, but the loss of this information poses an interpretative problem that we cannot resolve with any confidence.

What follows is a brief sketch of some of the possible directions in which a context-specific reading might take us.

If the play was produced shortly after the abandoned invasion by Pleistoanax in 446 and the negotiation of the subsequent truce (the 'Thirty Years' Peace'), it was probably performed – either at the Lenaia in January or at the City Dionysia in March – in the year 445, at a relatively high point in Athenian affairs after a series of defeats and forced concessions. Thucydides' account (1.114) is brief and dry but the acuity of the situation is evident. The Spartan invasion was a critically timed move, and apparently a surprise one. Following significant Athenian losses in Boeotia and the concession of territorial control there, the bulk of the Athenian forces, led by Pericles, was north in Euboia putting down another major revolt. While there they heard that Megara – an important city near Athens – had also revolted and killed the Athenian garrison. While Pericles was returning to Megara, the Spartan force invaded, creating a third simultaneous military front. The termination of the Spartan attack allowed the Athenians to focus on regaining Euboia, and the brokering of the Peace promised a period of recovery and growth after years of a war which had recently been going badly.

If this – the end of the first Peloponnesian War – is the context of our play's production we can understand the play as a celebration not of martial spirit or prowess but of peace. This resonates with the tone of the first and third choral odes (353–80, 748–83), which repeatedly praise the moral and artistic accomplishments of Athens rather than its military power (e.g. 'great Athens with her beautiful dances', 359–60, and the description of the Panathenaea festival at 777–83), and hope to avert war, reproaching Eurystheus for seeking it out (e.g. 'but, oh lover-of-war, don't disrupt the city that is full of graces with your spear, but hold back!' 378–80, 'send elsewhere the man who is unjustly leading his spear-brandishing army here from Argos' 773–5). It also transforms the way in which we read the arming scene of

Iolaus; in wartime his determination to fight is admirable, but in peacetime his ambition may take on more of the ludicrous quality that centres primarily on his infirmity. The ending may also take on greater urgency; appropriate behaviour in the aftermath of war would be a pressing concern.

If the play was produced at the beginning of the second Peloponnesian War, the range of possible contexts broadens. The earliest probable date, with Eurystheus' prophecy anticipating a Spartan invasion, is approval for production in 432 and performance at the Lenaia in January 431.[7] According to Thucydides (1.119–26), Sparta and its allies met in the summer of 432 and voted to go to war, declaring that Athens had violated the conditions of the Peace earlier that year. They then spent almost a year making preparations during which a series of demands was exchanged between Sparta and Athens, including war as a consequence for not answering various charges (1.139). Conflict was impending, and a poet writing in 432 could certainly have anticipated a Spartan invasion, as would an audience in early 431. In this context, the construction of responsibility for the war is highlighted, and particularly the contrast between Argive aggression and Athenian justice and piety. At the same time, the anticipation of the attack, expressed in the songs of the chorus (353–80, 748–83) and Demophon's anxiety (381–424), becomes much more resonant, reflecting the contemporary Athenian state of awaiting an invasion with mingled confidence and apprehension. Iolaus' determination to fight regardless of his infirmity becomes a model to be emulated, and Eurystheus' prediction becomes a warning and a reproach to the Spartans.

If the play was approved in 431 and performed in 430, it was written in the year after the first invasion. Thucydides describes the Athenian preparations (2.14–17) as citizens from the countryside left their homes and took shelter in the city, 'each doing nothing less than abandoning his own city' (2.16). Most had no specific hosts, but settled wherever they could, including 'the sanctuaries and hero-shrines' (2.17). The audience of 430 had seen a Peloponnesian army follow more or less the same route taken by Euripides' Eurystheus,[8] and had seen Athenian lands ravaged and Pericles blamed for it (2.21) – in terms not dissimilar to the criticism of Demophon in our play when the people hear of the oracle requiring a sacrifice (415–19). The Athenians had in turn invaded the region around Megara in the fall, and had heard the famous public funeral orations for the dead over the winter. While Thucydides' version of Pericles' speech was written some time later and detailed comparison would be unproductive, there are many points of contact between the Athenian characteristics singled out for praise in Thucydides (2.36–42) and throughout Euripides' *Children of Heracles.* It is even possible that by March, when the plays were performed at the City Dionysia, citizens from the surrounding lands in Attica would already have moved inside the Athenian walls; if not, the move was impending. The audience of 430 would not only be braced for another Spartan invasion; it would have been keenly sensitive to the plight of fugitives and the impact on the distant kin who received them, and conflicted as to their leader.

What is more, in the summer of 431 the Plataeans, Athenian allies to the northwest, successfully defended themselves against a Theban attack and took hundreds of captives, using these as hostages to persuade a reinforcing army to withdraw. When the Athenians were informed of this situation, they sent a herald to their ally telling them not to kill the prisoners (yet), but by the time the herald arrived the Plataeans had already killed the Theban captives, possibly in spite of an oath swearing that they would spare them if the Theban reinforcements withdrew (Thuc. 2.2–6).[9] The parallels with the final scene of the play are strong, and the audience of 430 would have particular reason to criticize Alcmene's behaviour and the chorus' compliance, perhaps even distancing the chorus of Marathonians as allies like the Plataeans rather than Athenians.

The Athenian situation became more acute still in the next two years. The year 430 included not only a much more destructive forty-day Spartan invasion but also the plague that devastated Athens shortly thereafter, and Thucydides gives us an extensive and vivid description of the whole city suffering 'with people dying inside and the land plundered outside' (2.54). In the summer of 429 Athens was not invaded, but suffered a second plague, which killed Pericles in the autumn; an audience in 428 may well have been more sensitive to the vacuum produced by the absence of powerful figures. What is more, if *Children of Heracles* was staged in 428, it was in all likelihood produced as part of the same tetralogy as *Hippolytus* at the City Dionysia festival – another play with important Athenian material, with another of Theseus' sons as the title character and Theseus himself onstage.

The year 427 is often put forward as the last probable date of the play's production since Wilamowitz-Moellendorff (1882a: xv) pointed out that the summer of that year saw the most extensive Spartan devastation of Attic land, including 'all that had been left alone in the previous invasions' (Thuc. 3.26), after which Eurystheus' prophecy might appear hollow.[10] This is, however, a weak *terminus ante quem*. If we accept that the idea of divine support gained particular meaning in the context of an ongoing war, there is no reason to assume that it would be considered to lose its value after a difficult year. Eurystheus does not promise that the Heraclids' descendants will be prevented from attacking, only that he will be their fiercest enemy when they do (1034–6). An audience later in the 420s might understand that (like other violators of divinely-backed *nomos*) the Spartans would be punished for transgressing the bond between suppliant and protector, without expecting that they would be prevented from doing so.

It is accordingly worth including 426 and later years in the possible range of dates for our play. After the Spartans withdrew from Attica in the summer of 427, Athens successfully put down a revolt in Mytilene on Lesbos, and the city debated fiercely over appropriate reprisals, resolving first to kill all men and sell all children and women into slavery, but eventually deciding to spare all but the ringleaders. The same year saw the massacre of the Plataeans – the same Athenian allies who killed their Theban hostages in 431 – after they surrendered to the Spartans. It also saw a terrible civil war in Athens' ally Corcyra (on the island of Corfu to the west of mainland Greece), where the atrocities included the killing of suppliants at an altar (Thuc. 3.81.5). And the winter of 427/6 saw yet another outbreak of the plague. For an audience of 426 many of the elements of *Children of Heracles*, but especially the debate over the treatment of a prisoner of war, would have had powerful and immediate resonance.

We could extend this speculation in breadth to other possible years and in depth of detail, but I think it has been made sufficiently clear that the context-specific readings are extremely rich for this play – so rich that they cannot be used to narrow down the possible dates. Fortunately, the play does not depend on its initial performance context for its power, and until we can discover new evidence it is more productive to turn to later performances and their contexts, and to consider how they can shape our understanding of the play.

A classical reperformance?

Theatre is an essentially ephemeral art form; once performed it leaves few if any material traces. We are fortunate that at least some records – mostly titles – have survived for quite a few of our ancient plays in addition to the extant texts, thanks to the popularity and civic importance of the genre. But plays written for the festivals of Athens were reperformed both there and in other parts of the Greek world during the fifth and fourth centuries BCE,[11] and there is some evidence to suggest that *Children of Heracles* was successfully reperformed in South Italy in the late fifth century BCE.

Written records for this kind of performance are even more limited and haphazard than our records for original performances, and we have none for *Children of Heracles*. We must therefore rely on indirect evidence and inference. One common line of argument draws on vase-paintings. If several vase-paintings related to a particular play can be traced back to the same approximate time and place of origin, we may infer that this is evidence of a reperformance influencing the local artisans. This is a tricky business. The extent to which we can confidently associate vase-paintings with specific tragedies rather than general mythological traditions is itself a matter of debate; while there are plenty of paintings that show genre-specific indicators for comedy, such as stages, masks and costumes, tragic representations are not marked in this way.[12] What is more, these paintings do not represent particular moments of a production; these days even scholars who are most confident of the link between vase-painting and tragedy accept that what is represented is 'informed by' rather than an illustration of a performance.

For *Children of Heracles*, some scholars point to the existence of two vase-paintings that seem to be closely linked to our play as evidence for a reperformance outside of Athens.[13] Both paintings contain details that are specific enough to our play to suggest Euripidean influence rather than a generic mythological scene. Both vases were produced in the last quarter of the fifth century BCE in Heraclea in the Lucanian region of South Italy (the 'instep' of the boot), a town founded in 433/2 officially as a colony of a Spartan settlement, Taras (modern Taranto), but in practice as a joint enterprise with an Athenian settlement, Thurii, as a compromise following a conflict over the territory.[14]

The first is a *pelike*, a two-handled jar used for transportation and storage.[15] (See Fig. 6.) The subject is usually identified as Iolaus – leaning against the altar column, carrying a suppliant branch and what seems to be a walking stick to hint at his age, though his hair and beard are neither white nor noticeably thinning, the most common

Fig. 6 Late fifth-*c.* BCE Lucanian *pelike*, 44.5 cm. Policoro, Museo Nazionale della Siritide.

signals of old age in vase-painting[16] – and four Heraclids wearing suppliant wreaths. They are grouped at a blood-stained altar, the outer two carrying suppliant branches and the inner two holding Iolaus' clothes. A fifth child, unwreathed, stands on Iolaus' shoulder; this figure is sometimes interpreted not as one of the Heraclids, but as having a symbolic significance. They face a herald (presumably Eurystheus') with Athena behind them. The scene corresponds well to the early scenes of our play, with Athena standing in conceptually for the city, the chorus and Demophon. The only discrepancy with our play (apart from Iolaus' hair and beard) is that the column on the altar supports a beardless cult statue (also looking at the Herald) that is very unlikely to be Zeus.[17] However, as Taplin points out (2007: 127),

Fig. 7 Late fifth-*c.* BCE Lucanian column-*krater*, 52 cm. Berlin, Staatliche Museen.

just as Zeus remains offstage in extant tragedy, he rarely appears on tragedy-related vases.

The second is a column-*krater*, a vessel for mixing water and wine.[18] (See Fig. 7.) This painting once again shows Iolaus (marked as an old man by his white hair and his staff) and two children at the altar, with a young Herald beside him.[19] The larger of the two children is turned away in a relaxed posture, while the men watch the arrival of a pair of horsemen. These can be plausibly interpreted as Demophon and Acamas, who are often depicted with horses,[20] which in this painting may also indicate the distance they have travelled, especially given that the upper figure is wearing a travelling hat. A woman sits behind the altar facing away from the action with a small statue of Zeus (carrying his thunderbolt) in her lap; she is usually identified as Alcmene, though her dark hair may suggest that this is the Daughter.[21] In either case, her position and the statue may suggest the seclusion of the women within the temple in the first part of the play. This cannot represent any single moment in the play – it is exceedingly unlikely that horses appeared on stage! – but each element can be constructively and persuasively interpreted as part of the play.

Neither of the paintings shows what might be considered a 'still' from our play, and in each case there are grounds for a skeptical viewer to deny a connection with Euripides' telling of the myth. Nevertheless, the prominent figures of the heralds in both paintings as well as the two riders and the disengaged woman in the second painting reflect important and distinctive features in Euripides' particular telling which do not form part of other traditions of which we are aware. I am therefore inclined to accept that there is indeed a connection between these paintings and the play. If we accept this identification, then we may reasonably ask why these two vase-paintings were produced in the same place at (as far as we can tell) approximately the same time, and we may reasonably answer that they were probably inspired by a local, late fifth-century production of our play.

We may finally return to the central question of this section. How might this context – a South Italian performance toward the end of the Peloponnesian War, in a town named for Heracles with mixed ties to both Athens and Sparta – have shaped the audience's reception of the play? Allan (2001b: 79–81 and n. 69) demonstrates that the affiliations of Heraclea were predominantly Spartan, and argues persuasively that the prominence of the Athenian figures on the vases demonstrates that the play's appreciation by the local audience was not unduly affected by a narrow political and partisan interpretation. Certainly the Athenian figures on the vases suggest that the play was not drastically altered to cater to perceived anti-Athenian biases. However, we must also keep in mind that vases of this kind were essentially for private rather than public use, and that while the town of Heraclea was primarily affiliated with pro-Spartan Taras, individuals may also have had deep-rooted Athenian connections through the Thurian settlers. To me, these vases suggest that the pro-Athenian material might have had special meaning for at least some of the audience. However, Allan is right to point out how striking it is that *Children of Heracles* was selected for performance in a pro-Spartan town in the late fifth century BCE. We know very little about the logistics such as repertoire selection of the production of drama outside of Athens, which must have varied from place to place – but at the very least we can say that its political content did not prevent the selection and production of this play.

Traces of modern performance: the Archive of the Performance of Greek and Roman Drama (APGRD)

When the works of ancient Greece and Rome were rediscovered and celebrated in the Renaissance, leading to the publication of the Greek text of Euripides' complete[22] work in 1503 (the Aldine edition) and a Latin version in 1541 (the Basel edition), *Children of Heracles* was of course included. But since the sixteenth century it has tended to be published – especially in translation – only as part of 'complete works' series together with other Euripidean plays. (Let us not forget that it is probably to such a series, alphabetically organized, that we owe its preservation in the first place.)

It has also been only rarely selected and adapted for performance. No complete data is available, but we can get a good sense of the relative popularity of ancient plays from the work of the APGRD, which since 1996 has been working to assemble and preserve records of productions. Their database of performances is not complete,[23] but it is an invaluable resource. As of January 2019, there are only twelve entries in the APGRD for performances related to Euripides' *Children of Heracles* – only twelve productions in the half-century covered by the archive. This is the lowest total for any extant Greek play.[24] Of those twelve, five are twentieth-century productions with limited audiences (and there are doubtless more of these that have not been recorded).

The dubious distinction of being Euripides' least-performed play comes with the advantage that it is possible for us to discuss all of the larger productions and to consider the contexts that produced them.

Eighteenth-century revival as romance: Danchet, Marmontel, Delap and the Daughter

To my knowledge *Children of Heracles* was not performed in modern times until 1695. The *Héraclides* of De Brie (16??–1713) was performed at the Comédie-Française in February of that year, but it was not an auspicious debut for our play's reception; the play received only six poorly attended performances, which was meagre for the time. No script has survived. The poet is almost entirely unknown apart from the entry in the records of the theatre, a few anecdotes and several very uncomplimentary witticisms by his contemporaries.[25] I have not been able to discover his year of birth or even his first name, but the anecdotal evidence suggests that he was a pupil, or perhaps merely an admirer, of the classicist André Dacier.

In 1719, twenty-six years after the failure of De Brie's play, the Comédie-Française put on a second *Héraclides* written by Antoine Danchet (1671–1748). The play was likewise not a success, as we can judge both from the theatre records for its eight performances and from contemporary comment.[26] However, Danchet (unlike De Brie) was a member of the Académie Française, and the script has been preserved with his other writings, including other classically-themed plays, though no others for which there is a Greek exemplar.[27] His play was originally titled *Hylus*,[28] and the action opens with Hylus' confession of love for Laodice, a daughter of Demophon, who has (before the play's opening) persuaded her father to accept the Heraclids. However, the play focuses on the Daughter of Heracles, called Astérie, who has been raised in Athens in ignorance of her birth, and who is in love with Hylus (not knowing he is her brother) but loved by Demophon. She eventually commits suicide, mistakenly thinking that Hylus is dead, and accidentally fulfils an oracular condition for victory (the shedding of Heraclid blood), leaving Hylus to marry Laodice. Danchet's focus on sensational love at the expense of the political and civic elements of Euripides' play is reflected in the cast changes; the other Heraclids and Alcmene are eliminated, and neither Eurystheus nor any representative of his appears onstage, but confidantes are added for each young woman.

Yet a third *Héraclides* was performed in the Comédie-Française in 1752, when Jean-François Marmontel (1723–99), a protégé of Voltaire, produced another adaptation. We are fortunate in possessing, in addition to the theatre records, both the script of the play as well as the author's reflections on it, which (used with caution) contain valuable insights.[29] This play was part of a short phase early in a varied and prolific intellectual career in which Marmontel produced five tragedies on classical themes in six years (1748–53). The first, *Denys le tyran* (centred on Dionysius of Syracuse), was well received, but his last play, *Egyptus*, was performed only a single time in 1753 and the text was never published. Our play is the only one of the five that draws its source material from an existing play, and he acknowledges his debt to Euripides in his reflections.

Marmontel's *Héraclides* was not a success; it ran for eight performances in May/June, and three more in November. The author's memoirs attribute its failure to a growing personal and professional enmity in theatrical and literary circles, as well as a catastrophic first performance in which (as he reveals in his memoirs, having suppressed it in his earlier discussion of the play) the lead actress accidentally became drunk.[30] In the same passage of his memoirs he also tells us that he chose the subject because he was looking for something 'more pathetic' than his preceding play *Cléopâtre*, and in this respect he was satisfied; he calls *Héraclides* 'the most feebly written of [his] plays, but the most pathetic', describing the emotional effect on his rehearsal audience and on 'the few people who saw it' after the disastrous opening. Importantly for our purposes, he also refutes rumours that he was influenced by Racine's *Iphigénie* of 1674, and comments on the similarity between Euripides' *Children of Heracles* and his *Iphigenia at Aulis*, noting the importance of the virgin sacrifice but emphasizing the difference between a 'commanded sacrifice' and a 'voluntary dedication' (1819: vi–vii). The Daughter (called Olympie) is certainly the centre of the play, and he replaces Alcmene with Heracles' widow Deianeira to create a focal mother-daughter relationship that seems to have reminded his critics of Euripides' Clytemnestra and Iphigenia. He also introduces almost from the beginning a son of Demophon (Sthenelus) as a love interest and heroic rescuer for Olympie. The play accordingly centres on Olympie's self-sacrifice, her mother and her lover. These changes reflect the kind of romantic focus used by Danchet, as well as the Renaissance interest in the figure of the virgin sacrifice.[31] Again, the political context is set to the side; Marmontel focuses instead on the suppliant and sacrifice patterns and resolves them in a new romantic ending.

Very similar changes are made in the next recorded adaptation of our play: *The Royal Suppliants,* produced in 1781.[32] This was an English adaptation of our play by John Delap (1725–1812), a Cambridge-educated churchman based in Sussex who had previously written a version of *Hecuba* as well as at least one other classically-themed play that was never produced or published. We have the script of Delap's play, two editions of which were published in the same year that it was performed, as well as some correspondence between the author and the producer, the influential David Garrick, which shows that a draft of the play was more or less complete in 1762.[33] The play ran for nine nights at Drury Lane, which was a respectable if not a profitable run, and there were further performances outside of London.[34]

The published script begins with a prefatory 'advertisement' as follows:

> It may perhaps be necessary to acquaint the reader, that Euripides has written a tragedy upon the same subject. In his *Heraclidae,* Macaria is sacrificed in the second act, and never afterwards mentioned; and *Acamas* is a mute. Indeed the whole conduct of this play is so entirely different from that of the Greek poet, that the author is hardly conscious to himself of having borrowed any thing more from him, than the general idea of the *Suppliants* taking refuge in the temple, and Macaria's voluntary offer of her own life.

As this description indicates, Euripides' play is significantly adapted, and Delap himself highlights the same two principal changes that we saw in Marmontel: the focus on Macaria and the invention of a romantic interest (this time Acamas, now a major role). Deianeira once again replaces Alcmene, and the ending (thanks to Garrick's advice) is a happy one, this time because of Hyllus' intervention. While some scenes are closely modelled on Euripides, such as the arrival of

Eurystheus' Herald (called Alcander in Delap's play), we can again see a focus on the emotional and character-driven elements of the story.[35]

The adaptations of Danchet, Marmontel and Delap all simplify the plot of the play and choose a single focal character of a popular type; political elements are excluded and the titles scarcely reflect the content of the plays. These adaptations reflect the aesthetic taste of the times, but their relative lack of success may be related to the incongruity of the adaptation of Euripides' play into a romance. It is also striking that for the three French playwrights, *Children of Heracles* is the only Greek play that inspired an adaptation. Danchet and Marmontel certainly had broad familiarity with classical literature, and for their other plays they drew their subjects from non-dramatic classical sources. It is perhaps more surprising still that the unknown De Brie chose this obscure play as the foundation for his only tragedy in 1695, well before the first French translation of the play was published in the 1780s.[36] Again, we must remember that none of the French adaptations met with success in the theatre, but we can at least say that our play had a unique appeal to these playwrights.

Twentieth-century Greece under oppressive regimes

Over 150 years passed before the next two known performances of the play, both in twentieth-century Greece and both produced in times of political crisis.[37] Unfortunately, minimal records survive; we have almost no material either documenting or discussing these two Greek performances. We must deduce what we can from the inherently suggestive contexts of these productions, and while this is not the place for a discussion of Modern Greek history some outlines are necessary.

Modern Greece was not recognized as an independent nation until 1828 and was correspondingly late in restaging ancient drama, beginning in the years leading up to independence from the Ottoman empire with performances of *Persians, Hecuba* and *Philoctetes* in 1817–18.[38] Such productions increased in frequency and importance over the nineteenth century. In 1936 the Prime Minister Ioannis Metaxas declared a state of emergency and established a totalitarian and nationalist regime that sought among other goals to promote a unified Greek culture. During this time outdoor performance began to be deliberately revived and reclaimed beginning in 1938 at Epidaurus. Metaxas' death in 1941 preceded Nazi invasion and occupation by a few months. Under Nazi occupation, theatre became a still more complex site of both censorship and counterculture.[39] All artistic media were recognized as an essential part of the Nazi program, theatre was well-funded, and Greek and Roman art were generally considered important aesthetic models. There was no unified policy or legislation controlling performances, but all theatres under occupation were required to report their programs, and most did not take risks.[40] Other plays produced in Athens by the National Theatre of Greece during this time-frame include *Medea* (1942) and *Hecuba* (1943), both mainstays of modern revivals.

It is in this general context that Kyriazis Charatsaris produced an *Irakleides* in 1943, playing the role of Eurystheus himself.[41] The performance took place in Thessaloniki, a significant Jewish centre from medieval times and before, and a major site of resettlement for ethnic Greeks from the former Ottoman empire in the aftermath of the Graeco-Turkish war in the 1920s. It took place in the aftermath of mass deportations of the Jewish population which began in March 1943. No detailed information about the production has survived, but it is difficult to ignore the resonance of our play in a place with a history of welcoming displaced people that had just witnessed the persecution and dislocation of a major section of the population. The play's selection is all the more surprising given that it was not part of the standard repertoire of classical plays being produced at the time, and that its patriotic and military themes are pro-Athenian while Nazi ideology idealized a version of Sparta.

In 1954–5 the interrupted revival of outdoor performances of ancient Greek drama was resumed under the auspices of the Athens and Epidaurus Festival which continues to be celebrated annually. In 1967 there was a coup in Greece that established a military dictatorship governed by a junta (often referred to as 'the Colonels') that lasted until 1974. Under this regime liberties of all kinds were curtailed, and theatre again became heavily controlled but also exploited by the resistance.[42] This was the context of the second production, also called *Irakleides*, directed by Lambros Kostopoulos for the National Theatre of Greece, performed at Epidaurus (1970 and 1971) and Athens (1971 and 1972).[43] Again, the details of the performance do not survive, and we can only speculate as to the balance of the pro-Athenian elements of the play and potentially subversive aspects, such as the downfall of the general Eurystheus.

Now, other ancient plays were revived under both of these regimes; *Children of Heracles* was the third production directed by Kostopoulos at Epidaurus under the military dictatorship, following *Medea* (1968, revived several times in subsequent years) and *Antigone* (1969).[44] What is striking is that it is *only* under these regimes that *Children of Heracles* has been selected by Greek directors, despite the formidable renewal of tragic performances in the last century. Furthermore, it was permitted by both the Nazi censors and the Colonels, and even seems to have secured sufficient approval to be performed in a subsequent year. The play was apparently considered at least not to be subversive and at most actively supportive of oppressive power structures. This is all the more surprising given the play's focus on the dislocated and disenfranchised, and especially the play's reception in recent years.

In our time: modern refugee crises

Children of Heracles continues to be performed only rarely, but there have been three recent productions that have reached a fairly broad audience.[45] The first was a production called *Die Herakliden* which was performed in September 1996 in Basel under the direction of Hans-Dieter Jendreyko.[46] This performance was based on a translation of the play, with additional text incorporated from other plays of Euripides as well as some choral lyrics (some performed in the original Greek) from Aeschylus' *Seven Against Thebes*, another play about a besieged city in which the chorus is considerably more agitated than in Euripides' play. Flashar (2009: 351) highlights the fact that Jendreyko's production was performed in what used to be the customs clearance hall of the Badischer Bahnhof (train station) in Basel, and is now a small theatre (since 2000 the Förnbacher Theatre). The station was then and continues to be the first point of call for many asylum seekers arriving through Germany in the northeast. The Heraclids were seated on suitcases, and through a window the audience could see members of the actual Swiss Border Guard; the space explicitly invited comparison of the Heraclids with modern refugees.

The next major production was the 2002–4 tour of the American Repertory Theatre, directed by Peter Sellars.[47] The production received considerable attention with reviews in a wide range of publications, and it continues to be frequently discussed in academic work.[48] The play was performed between November 2002 and January 2003 in Bottrop (Germany), Rome, Paris and Boston, with a second European tour in May to June 2004, taking in Antwerp, Amsterdam and Barcelona. It was an extremely socially engaged investigation of the modern refugee crisis, explicitly framed by panel discussions with policy makers and relief workers before the play, and films and other artistic presentations by refugees afterwards, with moderators remaining on stage during the performance of the play. The choral songs were replaced by a single musician (Ulzhan Baibussynova) performing Kazakh folk tunes and sitting on the 'altar' space where the Heraclids were gathered, and the choral lines within the episodes were distributed to audience members, overtly demanding a form of civic engagement. During the European tour this also created a multi-lingual play as the actors performed in English with surtitles, but the choral lines were delivered in the local language. The silent group of Heraclids at the altar were played by local teenage refugees who entered the seating area twice to shake hands with the audience – once during the scene following the acceptance of the supplication when this is indicated by the text (307–8), and again after the account of the battle and the announcement of the Athenian victory, after which they left the stage. The costumes were modern and Western, with Iolaus' infirmity emphasized by a wheelchair, but Alcmene was swathed in long dark fabric to create a vaguely Middle Eastern effect. The ending of the play framed Eurystheus as an unrepentant dictator, appearing in an orange jumpsuit (behind plexiglass in some productions, with an echoing sound effect to give the effect of a reported trial); this framing deliberately recalled modern war-crime trials from Nuremberg to the then-ongoing trial of Milošević. The ambiguity of the ending was downplayed.

The most recent larger-scale production was a *Children of Hercules* directed in 2005 by Phil Willmott (who also played Demophon), using Kenneth McLeish's translation. This was a free performance in the Scoop, an outdoor theatre in London seating approximately 800 that has been putting on Greek and other plays since 2003.[49] *Children of Hercules* was produced in a double bill with *Treasure Island.* This startling pairing contrasts strongly with Sellars' companion elements, and reflects the company's ambition to reach and engage a broad audience, as do other elements such as the staging of a fight scene between the rejuvenated Iolaus and Eurystheus. At the same time, the costumes emphasized the refugee aspect of the play, with the suppliants dressed as gypsies and some actors in the uniforms of British immigration officers. The ambiguity of the ending was emphasized, with the final question of the justice of Alcmene's wish for vengeance thrown open to the audience and left unanswered.

Each of the three contexts we have considered has engaged with *Children of Heracles* in a very different way. The eighteenth-century adaptations reshaped Euripides' play as a foundation for almost entirely original and apolitical work which went generally unappreciated. In twentieth-century Greece, the play seems to have been (made?) acceptable to the totalitarian regimes under which it was produced, despite its unique investigation of unconventional power dynamics. More recent productions have only lightly adapted Euripides' text, and have emphasized the political themes that resonate with contemporary refugee crises. Even this brief description of the play's reception history demonstrates how rich its theatrical potential is, and how diverse – if sporadic – its life on stage has been.

Children of Heracles in the hands of scholars

I turn at last and briefly to the most specialized and the most devoted of Euripides' audiences: the academic community. Even here reception of *Children of Heracles* has been neither extensive nor enthusiastic. The 'mutilation' of the play's text was suggested early in the nineteenth century by Hermann, and its negative assessment was entrenched by the eminent scholar Ulrich von Wilamowitz-Moellendorf through the publication of two critical articles in 1882 (now both reprinted in his *Kleine Schriften*). This view influenced many others scholars in the decades that followed, until Zuntz' defence of the text in 1947 and of the quality of the play in the first edition of his monograph in 1955.

Since then, most scholars have strongly rejected the earlier negative assessment; however, virtually all of them allow it to colour their own readings by opening with an overview of increasingly outdated judgements. Where the tone of older (nineteenth- and early twentieth-century) scholarship on the play has been damningly critical or dismissive, recent scholarship has been almost as damningly defensive. I have tried to avoid this approach.

There are some excellent articles and book chapters on *Children of Heracles*, as described in the Guide to Further Reading below. However, the play has remained as far outside of the scholarly mainstream as it has been outside of mainstream theatre repertoire. It is striking that since Zuntz' monograph it has almost always been discussed in conjunction with Euripides' *Suppliant Women*; the play has very rarely been an independent focus of investigation as compared to other Greek tragedies. Not even all of these focused studies have been wholehearted. Consider, for example, the opening of the preface to the 1907 student commentary written by the English scholar Alfred Pearson (1861–1935): 'This book has been written at the request of the Syndics of the Cambridge University Press, who were of opinion that the time had come for a new edition of the *Heraclidae*.'[50]

However, I note with optimism that the play (and scholarship on it) is increasingly being integrated into wider discussions of the playwright and the genre. As a superficial but suggestive measure of this, the indexes of broad discussions of Euripidean tragedy – those organized thematically rather than play-by-play – show that where *Children of Heracles* was scantily represented in much of the work of fifty years ago, in recent studies such as Walton's *Euripides our Contemporary* (2009) and Mastronarde's *The Art of Euripides* (2010) it receives the same attention as any other play.[51] As the play receives increasingly even-handed treatment by scholars, it is more likely to reach a correspondingly broader public audience.

Epilogue

Children of Heracles is a powerful play, and its power can be amplified by the specific context of its performance. At the same time, it does not need to be anchored to a particular time and place to captivate and challenge its audiences. Its appeal depends on the appreciation of the variety of tones, themes and characters presented, and in their careful juxtaposition and interaction as each element is displaced only to re-emerge in a new light. Euripides uses the compression and layering of the plot to create depth and complexity from deceptively simple examples of familiar patterns. Attempts to isolate a 'key' to *Children of Heracles* – a character, or a plot structure or even Greek concepts such as *nomos* and *charis* – can be illuminating but are ultimately even less satisfactory for our play than they are for most. Recognizing the changeability of its focus is key to appreciation of the play, as well as appreciation of the broad range of audiences for whom it carries meaning.

Appendix: Fragments

In addition to the main text of the play that has been preserved in medieval manuscripts, there are five fragments that have been attributed to the play but that are not included in the transmitted text. It is now the majority opinion among scholars that these fragments do not in fact belong to our play, but the question is not settled and the possibility has been accepted as recently as 1993.[1] It is not the aim of this appendix to summarize the whole debate, but simply to provide the fragments for assessment.

All of the fragments are in iambic trimeter, the metre that is generally used in episodes rather than sung by the chorus in odes or by actors in moments of extreme emotion. Our sources for the first four fragments are Stobaeus and Orion, both fifth-*c.* CE anthologists who collected quotations from classical poetry and prose. Working 800 years after our play was written, in Macedon and Egyptian Thebes respectively, it is almost certain that they relied for much of their material on earlier collections. The last quote is a line from a comedy by Aristophanes, a contemporary of Euripides who often parodied his work.

1. Nauck/Kannicht fragment 852: 'Whoever honours his parents in life, this man is dear to the gods in his life and when he dies. Whoever is not willing to honour his parents may not join me in sacrificing to the gods or set out to sea in a shared ship.' Stobaeus (4.25.2) and Orion (*flor. Eur.* 7). Stobaeus quotes only the first sentence, naming our play as its source, while Orion gives both sentences but does not mention the source play. It is possible that the two sentences do not belong together, as Orion does not clearly separate his quotations.
2. Nauck fragment 949, Kannicht 852a: 'and to give due honour to their parents.' Stobaeus (4.25.3) and Orion (*flor. Eur.* 9).

3. Nauck/Kannicht fragment 853: 'There are three virtues which you
   must practice, child: to honour the gods and those who raised you
   and the common laws of Greece. By doing these things you will
   have the fairest crown of glory forever.' Stobaeus (3.1.80).
4. Nauck/Kannicht fragment 854 (with two versions of the second
   line): 'To die as a sacrifice is terrible, but brings fame.

   a) Not to die is cowardly (*de deilon*), and there is pleasure in it.'
      Plutarch *On Moral Virtue* (*Moralia* 447E).
   b) Not to die is not terrible (*oude deinon*), and there is pleasure in
      it.' Stobaeus (3.7.8).

   Plutarch (first *c.* CE) gives no source for this fragment; in Stobaeus
   it is attributed not to *Children of Heracles* but to Euripides'
   Heracles, which also does not include this line in the transmitted
   manuscript. It was reassigned to this play by Nauck because of the
   reference to sacrifice, which has some resonance with the
   Daughter's words at 562, 'I am going to the horror (*to deinon*) of
   sacrifice,' particularly with Stobaeus' reading.
5. Nauck/Kannicht fragment 851: 'stir up and make mincemeat of
   the business.' This is line 214 from Aristophanes' *Knights*, which
   an old commentary (perhaps as early as the third *c.* BCE) tells us
   is a parody of an iambic line from Euripides' *Children of Heracles*,
   but without specifying which line.

Selected Chronology

Key:

Publication as part of complete edition of Euripides
    Individual edition (Greek text and/or vernacular commentary)
      Performance

Chronology:

1503: first complete Greek text (Aldine edition, Venice)
1541: first complete Latin translation (Basel edition)
    1627: produced for Jesuits (Paris)
      1694–5: French adaptation by De Brie (Comédie-Française, Paris)
      1719–20: French adaptation by Danchet (Comédie-Française, Paris)
1743–54: first complete Italian translation by Carmeli (Paduà)
      1752–3: French adaptation by Marmontel (Comédie-Française, Paris)
      1781: English adaptation by Delap (London/Bath)
1781: first complete English translation (vol. 1; 1783 vol. 2) by Potter (London)
1782: second complete English translation by Wodhull (Cambridge)
1783: first complete French translation by Prévost (expansion of Brumoy's *Le Théâtre des Grecs*)
1800: first complete German translation by Bothe (Berlin)
    1813: with Latin commentary by Elmsley (Oxford)
    1907: with English commentary by Pearson (Cambridge)
      1943–4: modern Greek, directed by Charatsaris (Thessaloniki)

1958: with Italian commentary by Garzya (Rome); second edition
in 1995

*1970–2: modern Greek, directed by Kostopoulos (Athens/
Epidaurus)*

1972: Greek text only, edited by Garzya (Teubner, Stuttgart)

1993: with English commentary by Wilkins (Oxford)

*1996: German-language Swiss production (Badischer Bahnhof,
Basel)*

2001: with English commentary and translation by Allan
(Warminster)

2002–3: American production (Boston with European tour)

2005: UK production (The Scoop, London)

Guide to Further Reading

Translations:

Prose with parallel Greek text: William Allan (2001a, see bibliography) and David Kovacs (1995, in *Euripides II*, Loeb Classical Library 484, Harvard University Press). Be aware that Kovacs supplies his own text and translation where he perceives a gap in the transmitted text, subtly marked by <angle brackets>.

Verse: Mark Griffith has written an excellent (and much-needed) new translation for the third edition of the complete University of Chicago Press translations (2013, in *Euripides I*). The idiom is modern but not aggressively so; similarly the metre is occasionally used flexibly but with a clear pentameter foundation. In keeping with the series style, sung verses are set in italics, which is a useful visual cue, and there are textual rather than interpretative notes.

For the stage: Henry Taylor and Robert A. Brooks collaborated on the translation for Oxford University Press's *Greek Tragedy in New Translations* (1981 in independent binding, or Volume III of *The Complete Euripides*), a series that brought together a poet and a classicist to produce a translation of each extant tragedy. This version is written for the stage in lively modern language and very loose verse, with plenty of stage directions. There is an enthusiastic introduction, ample notes and a glossary.

Kenneth McLeish's translation for Bloomsbury's Methuen Classical Drama series (1997, in *Euripides Plays 5*) also has the stage in mind, with colloquial English and very loose verse. This was the translation chosen by Willmott for the 2003 performance at the Scoop, London.

Prose: John Davie's Penguin translation (1996, in *Euripides: Medea and other Plays*, London) is in prose, with the odes emphatically elevated into verse. There are useful notes by Richard Rutherford, as well as an introduction.

Robin Waterfield's for OUP's Oxford World's Classics series (2017, in *Euripides: Heracles and other plays*) is prose throughout. There are useful notes by James Morwood, and an introduction by Edith Hall.

To my knowledge there is no published translation of the play that is not part of a complete set (though the Taylor and Brooks is available in an independent binding), nor one produced by a woman.

Commentaries

For those without Greek, Allan's commentary (2001a) includes a parallel English translation along with the Greek text and has a great deal to offer both general and scholarly audiences. For those learning Greek, Ambrose's commentary (1990) is very useful for intermediary students; for those with Greek, Wilkins (1993) is more philologically focused.

Scholarly work

I recommend beginning with two articles from the 1970s, each of which presents a reading of the play as a whole, which take opposing views of the ending, and which were produced simultaneously and so do not engage explicitly with each other:

Burian (1977), who reads the play as a movement from heroic idealization to fantasy to a realistic or logical correction.

Burnett (1976), who focuses on the concept of *nomos*. The same basic interpretation underlies the relevant chapter of her 1998 book, though the central argument is different.

I would then recommend any of the following:

Zuntz (1955/1963), one of the first modern appreciations of the play and still very useful.

Mendelsohn (2002), ch.1 provides an important introduction to the gender and political framework; ch. 2 is a sensitive reading of the play, structured as a running commentary.

Fitton (1961), still an excellent literary comparison of our play with *Suppliant Women.*

Roselli (2007), a lengthy article, with a refreshing Marxist reading of the Daughter scene, including many valuable discussions of earlier scholarship.

Conacher (1967:109–20), a good example of an attempt to read the play through a single theme (*charis*).

Tzanetou (2012, ch.3), an examination of the specifically Athenian implications of the play, with a primary focus on the suppliant and sacrifice scenes.

Marshall (1998), a brief discussion with insights gained from a recent theatrical production.

Wyles (2015), the first discussion of the play's reception.

Notes

Chapter 1

1   For a concise history of the transmission of Euripides' text see Mastronarde (2017), especially pp. 20–1 on the alphabetic plays. For a specialist account focused on the transmission of our play see Magnani (2000).

2   For a more detailed discussion of the date and of the issues of interpretation arising from it, see Chapter 5 pp. 87–96.

3   For a detailed study of the audience and its varied composition see Roselli (2011).

4   Burnett (1998: 156–7) speculates that *Children of Heracles* may have been, like *Alcestis*, a fourth play performed in place of a satyr-play.

5   The bibliography on staging and space is immense. The evidence for the physical theatre is accessibly laid out in Csapo/Slater (1995, ID and the final plates); see Ley (2007) for a study infused with practical experience.

6   For the importance of this question for Greek tragedy, see Van Erp Taalman Kip (1990, ch. 2), who distinguishes audience knowledge (which is important to our understanding of the play and which we can reasonably hope to reconstruct) from audience response (which we can only speculate about; see her chapter 5). For a sound investigation of the issue of audience knowledge from the perspective of historical and economic evidence, see Revermann (2006).

7   See Burian (1997).

8   The earliest surviving reference to the story is a fragment from the sixth/fifth-century historian and geographer Hecataeus of Miletus, who recounts that the Heraclids were turned away from Trachis by King Ceyx after Heracles' death (*FrGrHist* 1 F 30). For other versions, see Gantz (1993: 463–6) and Schmidt (1988).

9   Parker (1984) gives a concise account of this evidence.

10 J. Hall (1997: 56–65) argues persuasively that these 'traditional' stories are the result of an at least partially conscious effort to define Dorian ethnicity rather than a reflection of historical population movements. See also Tzanetou (2012, esp. ch. 3) and Grethlein (2003, esp. ch. 8) for the importance to the construction of Athenian identity of stories in which Athens protects the weak.

11 It is accessibly collected by Csapo/Slater (1995: 105, 109–110). There is no evidence for or against a *proagōn* at the Lenaia festival.

12 For discussion of how and when play titles were established see Sommerstein (2010) and Kaimio (2000).

13 It is remotely possible that there was another play by this name written by one Pamphilus, otherwise unknown; see the scholiast on Aristophanes' *Wealth* 385.

14 On the size of the chorus see Sansone (2016) with bibliography.

15 The exact placement of the altar is uncertain; see e.g. Rehm (1988) and Poe (1989).

16 For an overview of the limited evidence that we have for tragic costume, see Wyles (2011, ch. 1–2 and appendix).

17 It is possible that costuming might have suggested his status, but there is at least some evidence that there was not a clear difference between the appearance of free men and slaves in Athens (Ps-Xenophon *Constitution of the Athenians* 10–12).

18 Cf. Mendelsohn (2002: 62–5 and bibliography at n.22). We may compare this with the conflation of Argos and Mycenae which occurs through this play and in other Greek mythology/literature.

19 This is the name given to Eurystheus' herald as early as Homer (*Il.* 15.639–52) and used in the list of characters given in the summary (*hypothesis*) transmitted in the manuscript, which was composed centuries after the play. Most scholars now recognize that this name is not Euripidean, though some continue to use it; see further Yoon (2012: 105–6).

20 Taplin (1977: 218–21) gives a clear summary of a more detailed German account of the *boē* by Schulze. For a discussion of the historical evidence for actual bystander intervention, see Sternberg (2006: 76–103).

21 A late source, Philostratus (second/third *c.* CE), records a tradition in which Eurystheus' herald Copreus was killed by the Athenians 'while he

was trying to drag the Heraclids from the altar' (*Lives of the Sophists*, 2.1.8). There is, however, no evidence that this tale was current in the fifth *c.* BCE, and in any case such an action could not take place onstage.

22 See Ley (2007: 51–2) and his figure 8 for possible staging after the arrival of the chorus.

23 For a brief overview and representative examples, see Rutherford (2012: 190–200); for bibliography see Dubischar (2017: 371).

24 This name, like 'Copreus' for the Argive Herald, is found in the manuscript's list of characters. Again, most scholars now recognize that this name is not Euripidean, though some continue to use it; see further Yoon (2012: 105–6).

25 He is identified by many as Servant, but as I have argued elsewhere (Yoon 2015) his costume probably identifies him as a herald.

26 For a discussion of Euripides' innovation in his account of Eurystheus' death see McDermott (1991: 127–8).

27 The scholiast to Pindar's Pythian 9.79 (137 in the old line numbering) – that is to say, a commentator writing about a sixth-*c.* poem centuries later – records two related traditions: that Iolaus was already dead when the Heraclids were persecuted by Eurystheus, and was allowed to come back to life to rescue them; and that (as in our play) he was old and then rejuvenated. In both accounts he dies after despatching Eurystheus.

28 For a brief overview and representative examples, see Rutherford (2012: 200–16); for bibliography see Dubischar (2017: 371).

29 The Greek, τὰ ἐξ ἡμῶν, is ambiguous; it can be literally rendered either as 'things as seen by us' or as 'things done by us' – that is to say, we can either emphasize the chorus' point of view (e.g. 'from our side of things,' Griffith 2013: 184) or the chorus' actions (e.g. 'our actions', Allan 2001a: 127). It is also possible that both senses are meant; I have chosen the most heavy-handed solution in combining the two, but the Greek is more subtle than this.

30 In a much later version of our story (Apollodorus 2.8.1) Eurystheus is beheaded by Hyllus and when the head is sent to Alcmene she drives

pins into its eyes. Compare Hecuba in the *Iliad* (e.g. 24.212–14) and Euripides' *Hecuba* and fragmentary *Alexander*, and Clytemnestra in most plays (though her maternal anger cannot be said to be her only motivation).

31 Almost all readings of the play support this comparison; Burnett is the only one who specifically resists these parallels (1976: 22–5).

32 In addition to this general difficulty, there is a specific problem that centres on line 1050, in which Alcmene orders Eurystheus' body be given to the dogs. If this is to be interpreted literally, it contradicts both her intention of giving the body to his relatives (1022–4) and the burial at Pallene leading to hero cult (1030–6). Scholars either remove or emend this reference, rationalize it or assume that lines have been lost that contradict this command. See Allan (2001a on 1052).

33 This was the standard view before Zuntz' crucial 1947 article defending the essential completeness of the play. For a clear summary of scholarly positions on the problem see Mendelsohn (2002: 6 n.8) with bibliography. Such a solution is likely to demand the exit of Hyllus' Herald and a quick change of costume for the actor; the accepted 'three-actor' convention of tragedy means that in our play as it stands there is no room for a new arrival. Starkey (2018) gives a good survey of bibliography on the subject, while challenging the rigidity of the convention.

34 Damen (2003) calculates that the average Euripidean 'French scene' – that is to say, a scene with the same set of onstage characters, including *deus ex machina* scenes – is only sixty-eight lines long; the exodos as transmitted could easily accommodate such a scene without noticeably affecting the play's proportions.

Chapter 2

1 This approach is similar to recent 'literary' readings, such as Goslin (2017) and the overall interpretation presented in Allan's 2001 commentary, both of which generally follow the reading of Burian

(1977). Compare also the character-focused readings of Burnett (1976 Part II) and Avery (1971).

2   In the Greek context we may compare Socrates' discussion of the ridiculous (τὸ γελοῖον) in Plato's *Philebus*, which includes the example of those who falsely believe in their physical strength and power (ῥώμη and δύναμις, 49c).

3   A similar suggestion is made by E. Hall (1997: 112).

4   See Zelnick-Abramowitz (2005: 135–40).

5   See Zelnick-Abramowitz (2005: 131–5).

6   At one end of the spectrum, see e.g. Burian's positive description (1977: 17–19). At the other end, see e.g. Burnett (1976: 22–5) who does not accept any positive characterization of Eurystheus or any negative characterization of Alcmene in this scene. (She glosses over the prophecy of the Heraclid invasion of Attica.)

7   For the possibility that Alcmene represents a familiar type of vengeful elderly woman see Falkner (1989, especially 123–6).

8   See e.g. Herodotus 6.52. For a brief survey of the status of various descendants of Heracles as city founders and first kings across the Greek world see Malkin (1994, ch. 1, especially 33–43); for greater detail see Huttner (1997: 43–64).

9   Political readings have come a long way from an older (nineteenth- and early twentieth-century) view of the play as an unambiguously pro-Athenian piece – a view which tends to overlook or sidestep the interpretative problems caused by the ending of the play. For example, Zuntz' influential interpretation depends on reading the final episode as Alcmene's 'confirmation *per negationem*' of 'deep tendencies, often obscure yet finally triumphant, towards the right, the just, and the noble' (1963: 51). For recent nuanced political interpretations see e.g. Tzanetou (2012, ch. 3), who maps the relationship between the Athenians and Heraclids onto the historical relationships between hegemonic Athens and its allies (although she omits the final capitulation of the chorus from her discussion); Grethlein (2003, ch. 8), who sees the early idealization of Athenian democratic identity compromised both by the handling of the sacrifice and the ending; and Mendelsohn (2002, ch. 2), who argues that 'masculine civic identity is enhanced through

interaction with the feminine' (48). Almost all such readings since 1955 pair and compare the play with Euripides' *Suppliant Women*, in part because of the influence of the first edition of Zuntz' monograph.

10 See e.g. Kaimio (1988).

11 For other readings of this refusal, see Burnett (1976: 15) and Mendelsohn (2002: 79).

12 See e.g. Burnett (1976: 10), Mendelsohn (2002: 87–9), Tzanetou (2012: 84–7).

13 E.g. Apollodorus *Bib.* 2.7.3; Diodorus Siculus 4.33.5; Pausanias 2.18.7 and elsewhere.

14 Compare Dhuga (2011: 70–2), who sees the chorus as taking Demophon's place as he fades from the action (but without discussing the implications for the play of the increased 'politico-ritual authority' that his reading proposes).

15 For the importance of this association see Mendelsohn (2002: 114–15).

16 I follow the now common assignment of these lines to Hyllus' Herald. However, the medieval manuscript L assigns these restraining lines to the chorus – unsurprising given the Athenian perspective of these lines. For fuller discussion see Wilkins (1993 on 961–72). Retaining the manuscript distribution involves the chorus much earlier; this effect was used by Sellars in his 2002–4 production of the play (see further Chapter 5 pp. 107–8).

17 We need not be concerned about the discrepancy between this and the account given by the Slave, who says that it was Iolaus (879–87) who chose to spare him on the battlefield – not to spare his life, but to allow Alcmene to share in his punishment. The disparity can be rationalized, but we can also easily accept the shift in perspective.

18 Bakewell (1999) makes a strong case for the specific political resonance of this word, though he overstates its implications.

19 See Konstan (2007: 198–200) for the importance of the distinction between personal and military enmity in this play and in Greek culture generally.

20 We may compare Zeitlin's claim that Argos is generally presented in Athenian tragedy as a redeemable city (1986, especially 118).

21 For evidence and judicious assessment of this tradition see Wright (2010).

22 The suppliant pattern described here is dependent on but distinguishable from the conventions of both public and private supplication; see further Chapter 4 pp. 63–7.

23 See e.g. Burian (1977: 7), Burnett (1976: 5–8).

24 It is certainly stated that they will continue to act as suppliants (344–5) at least during the conflict with Argos, and they stay onstage and essentially grouped around the altar until the final exit. This effect may be enhanced if they retain their garlands and suppliant branches.

25 In tragedy we may compare Eteocles' exit at *Phoenissae* 779–83, and the similar scene in *Sept.* which may contain an onstage arming after 675–6. The importance of arming scenes in the *Iliad* has been a staple of Homeric scholarship since at least the 1930s; for an early English-language example see e.g. Armstrong (1958).

Chapter 3

1 Compare Avery (1971), who extends the Heraclid identity to include 'all those whose moral outlook and whose sense of responsibility have been affected by the lessons and examples contained in Heracles' career' (539).

2 This phrase is not distinct in the Greek word 'Heraclidae', a patronymic akin to our Donaldson, McDonald and MacDonald. Mendelsohn (2002: xiii–xiv) notes that 'Sons of Heracles' would be a more accurate translation than the conventional 'Children of Heracles'.

3 On doubling see Mendelsohn (2002: 56–7), Burnett (1976: 5 n.4). For an unusual reading of Eurystheus' relationship to Heracles see Pozzi (1993), who argues that Eurystheus functions in the final scene as 'a surrogate of Heracles' (34–5).

4 De Jong's 1991 monograph on the Euripidean messenger speech introduced the principles of narratology – the study of the role of the narrator in shaping the perspective and effects of an account – into mainstream discussion of Greek tragedy; for further bibliography see Dubischar (2017: 371).

5 The phenomenon of characterization in general and the degree to which it exists in Greek tragedy are subjects of considerable discussion;

see most recently e.g. de Temmerman/van Emde Boas (2018) and bibliography.

6   One striking omission is the madness during which he killed his wife Megara and their children, which Euripides dramatized in *Heracles*; the details of his death are also omitted.

7   This is a standard usage of *ekeinos* (see e.g. the standard Greek lexicon by Liddell, Scott and Jones under '*ekeinos*' usage I.2 'to denote well-known persons'). The construction is awkward in English and this subtlety is generally lost in translation.

8   In doing so he contradicts the earlier dismissive words of his own Herald ('these [children] grown to manhood would fight poorly against the armed Argives,' 171–2).

9   E.g. Menelaus at *Andromache* 519–22, Polymestor at *Hecuba* 1138–44, Lycus at *Heracles* 168–9, Odysseus at *Troades* 723. We can also compare the exposure of various heroes as infants, where the attempted killing is prompted by a specific prophecy rather than a general expectation of inheritance (see further Huys 1995). We can contrast the malicious killing (offensive rather than defensive) of children with living parents, such as Atreus' killing of his brother Thyestes' children, or Medea's and Procne's double-edged killings of their own children.

10 See e.g. Burian (1977: 7–10), Burnett (1976: 151–7), Avery (1971: 540–4).

11 This may be a loaded term for an Athenian audience; Papadodima (2014) points out the democratic importance of lot-drawing, and the tension between this process and the heroic values of the Daughter in this scene and of Ajax in Sophocles.

12 My translation takes advantage of an ambiguity permitted by the Greek syntax; most translators render this roughly as 'what has happened here is worthy of her father and of her noble birth.'

13 For a very different interpretation of the function of her gender and anonymity see Roselli (2007: 126–37).

14 For example, at *Odyssey* 11.601–29 Odysseus speaks in the underworld with 'the image' (εἴδωλον) of Heracles, while Heracles himself (αὐτός) is on Olympus, though the underworld 'image' is presented as a fully sentient figure.

15 Diodorus 4.57–8 (first *c.* BCE) and Pausanias 1.32.6 (second *c.* CE).

16 Compare e.g. Avery (1971: 546–50), Wilkins (1990: 332–3).

17 Perhaps the most striking omission from Theseus' story given our play's focus is that of his reception of Heracles as a suppliant, corresponding to the omission of the precursor episode of Heracles' madness; cf. p. 128 n.6. There is reason to believe that some text has been lost after line 217; see Wilkins (1993: 79–80). It is possible that either the Amazon or underworld adventures were elaborated, or that further exploits were listed.

18 For this shift in Theseus' importance see e.g. Mills (1997), who emphasizes consistent elements in his portrayal over time, and Walker (1995), who emphasizes contradictions and tensions in his development.

19 See e.g. Mills (1997: 97–104) on Euripides' management of this problem through Theseus in *Suppliant Women*; for the problem more generally see Ober (1989: 259–61). Compare Mendelsohn's interpretation of the conflation of Marathon and Athens (2002: 63–5); he sees this geographical blurring as part of a broad contemporary strategy by which aristocratic heroic values centred on kin (*genos*) are integrated into and subordinated to civic values centred on the *polis*. For a critique of contrasting heroic past and democratic present as over-looking the reality of class distinctions in fifth-century Athens, see Roselli (2007: 124).

20 The reverse may be just as true; for a discussion of Demophon's limitations see e.g. Garzya (1958: 23), and for political interpretations of these limitations see e.g. Burnett (1976: 9–10), Mendelsohn (2002: 87–9), Grethlein (2003, ch. 8).

21 There is some historical evidence for the use of representative champions; Herodotus (1.82) recounts that in 546 BCE the Argives and Spartans agreed to settle a territorial dispute by electing 300 soldiers from each side to fight on their behalf. The outcome was itself disputed, and Thucydides (5.41) tells us that during the Peloponnesian War, in 420 BCE, the Argives and Spartans negotiated a treaty that included the possibility of a similar rematch over the same territory.

22 For violence (*bia*) as the Herald's 'leitmotif' see Burian (1977: 6).

23 It is even possible that he arrives onstage as an old man; see Chapter 4, pp. 81–2.

24 A third option, ransom, was rare. See fuller discussion of Eurystheus' position at pp. 70–3.

Chapter 4

1   On the likelihood of an independent Theban/Boeotian tradition of
    Iolaus, see West (2009). See further Kron (1981). Alcmene, like many
    other women in Greek mythology, is always defined by her son and
    lover.

2   See Dickin (2009, chapters 1 and 4).

3   See Chapter 1 p. 8 with n.19 on the Argive Herald's
    anonymity.

4   For a different and insightful reading of these three examples, see
    Burnett (1976, part I), who focuses on the conflict of different aspects
    of human and divine law in each case.

5   For an overview of the *fugas* see Forsdyke (2005, ch. 6). This term is
    commonly rendered in English as 'exile'; however, I prefer 'refugee' not
    only because of its contemporary resonance and its shared root (*fug-*),
    but because it gives the correct sense of agency for our play. 'Exile' is a
    better translation when banishment is imposed by a political power, but
    in our play Eurystheus has not exiled the Heraclids; they have fled from
    Argos to escape death. The Greek encompasses both translations and in
    many cases it is not clear whether a *fugas* has been ordered to leave or
    has chosen to do so.

6   Literally 'one who comes,' ἱκέτης from the root ἱκνέομαι. See Gould
    (1973: 90–4) for the similar relationship between strangers (*xenoi*) and
    suppliants.

7   Gould (1973) is the seminal article for this topic, and Naiden (2006) the
    most comprehensive study. For a study of the visual evidence for this
    ritual, see Pedrina (2017).

8   See also Wilkins (1993 on 70), Mendelsohn (2002: 60–2); compare the
    more specific interpretation of the altar by Rosivach (1978).

9   See e.g. Burkert (1985: 59), Parker (1983: 182–3 on the altar and
    160–70 on sacred space more generally). Naiden (2006: 36–8)
    downplays the protective aspect of the altar and focuses instead
    on practical reasons for supplication at an altar instead of a direct
    approach to a powerful person: convenience, visibility and
    accessibility.

10 The details of how this was done vary according to the account. In Herodotus (5.71) they are simply 'removed' from the altar; in Thucydides (1.126) they are told they will be spared and treacherously killed. In Plutarch (*Life of Solon*, 12) they are persuaded to stand trial and attach a cord to the statue of Athena to claim her protection, but the cord breaks and the Athenians immediately kill them.

11 This is the threat – suicide at the altar – by which the suppliants in Aeschylus' *Suppliant Women* finally compel Pelasgus (455–73). See Parker (1983: 34–40 on the pollution of death in general; 183–5 on death of suppliants at an altar in particular).

12 A more ambiguous case is the divine pursuit of Orestes by the Furies in *Eumenides*, first at the altar of Apollo and then at the altar of Athena. They do not lay hands on him in the play, but it is noteworthy that at both altars the presiding god disrupts a direct action, Apollo putting the Furies to sleep and Athena interrupting the 'binding spell' that they are performing.

13 Naiden (2006) lists all examples of supplication in major Greek authors with their outcomes in Appendix 1a.

14 Cf. Gould (1973: 75): 'there is both a parallelism of function and a network of resemblances between the two.' Naiden (2006: 4 and throughout) articulates four elements in the process common to both contexts: a physical approach, a distinctive gesture, a verbal request and a response from the person supplicated.

15 For the historical herald see Mosley (1973, especially 84–92).

16 See Sealey (1976) on the question of this story's historicity.

17 Cf. e.g. Goblot-Cahen (1999), Burnett (1998: 148). For the connection of these two immunities in historiography, see Griffith (2008).

18 See Ducrey (1999, ch. 9) for Greek practice in general; for a focus on the Peloponnesian War see Panagopoulos (1985: 51–3, a summary of the conclusions of a 1978 monograph). A different approach is taken by Burnett (1976: 12) who reads 963–4 as distinguishing general custom (the *nomos* that Alcmene asks about) from a specific Athenian decree (in her interlocutor's reply).

19 See Ducrey (1999, ch. 10). We can add to the literary accounts archaeological sites such as that of Himera in Sicily, where a mass

fifth-century grave was recently excavated that seems to contain bodies of the defeated defenders (Vassallo 2010: 54).

20 Doubts have been raised as to the sense and text of 1015, in which Eurystheus claims that he must be called *gennaios* (noble) and *prostropaion* (lit. 'turning towards', often applied to suppliants including polluted persons supplicating for purification); see the commentaries of both Allan and Wilkins on 1014–15 for summary of the arguments and defence of the transmitted text.

21 It is possible to interpret the invitation as an ironic phrase; however, the seriousness of the prophecy that he reveals and the shift to the future tense makes this unlikely to be the tone of the whole speech.

22 Mikalson (1991: 34–5) rightly notes that the heroization is not presented as a benefit in itself. On the concept of the 'enemy hero' see e.g. Sourvinou-Inwood (2003: 324–5), Kearns (1989: 46–53), and the list of examples (of variable relevance) in Visser (1982).

23 There is, however, no independent evidence (i.e. inscriptions or literary references) for a cult of Eurystheus in the fifth century. For a survey of Euripidean cult aetiologies with a focus on the extent of poetic invention see Scullion (1999–2000, 222–4 on our play), and the counter-arguments of Seaford (2009).

24 Cf. Sourvinou-Inwood (2003: 323), Wilkins (1993 on 1026–44). We may compare the revelations of e.g. Polymestor in *Hecuba*.

25 Scholarly interest in this phenomenon has increased dramatically since the 1990s; for a general overview see Bonnechere/Gagné (2013), for tragedy the succinct summary in Marshall (2015), and their bibliographies. It is difficult to capture in English the neutrality of the Greek words for the person or animal sacrificed. The usual phrase 'sacrificial victim' brings with it an emphasis on vulnerability and innocence which is not always appropriate; cf. Mylonopoulos (2013: 64).

26 In 1991 the headless remains of an adult male from the late eighth *c.* BCE were discovered in Crete next to a funeral pyre in a possibly sacrificial context, of which Stampolidis (2015) is the most accessible publication. In August 2016 the culture ministry of Greece announced that an adolescent skeleton from the eleventh *c.* BCE has been

discovered in a stone-lined grave near a sacrificial altar of Zeus during current excavations on Mt Lykaion (lykaionexcavation.org/site/research-highlights, accessed November 2018). The site has yet to be fully excavated and the interpretation of this find is still unclear – as of January 2019 it has not yet been published in an academic context – but the discovery has excited speculation because Mt Lykaion is specifically associated in ancient sources with the sacrifice of young boys (Romano/Voyatzis 2014: 571–3 and n. 4). There is stronger (but still contested) evidence for human sacrifice in nearby contemporary cultures such as Carthage in North Africa; see e.g. Xella et al. (2013) with bibliography.

27 See Mylonopoulos (2013), who notes that 'Greek myths involving human sacrifice inspired far more Etruscan and Roman artists than Greek sculptors or vase painters' (62).

28 A notable exception is found in Plutarch (second *c.* CE), who tells us that the Athenian general Themistocles, on the advice of a seer and at the demand of the people, sacrificed three Persians to Dionysus before the battle of Salamis in 480 BCE (*Life of Themistocles* 13.2). He names the philosopher Phanias of Lesbos (fourth *c.* BCE) as his source.

29 See Gibert (2003: 161–7) for the 'sacrificial metaphor' in general.

30 On the date of the play see Chapter 5 pp. 87–91. It is worth noting that there are parallels for both of these types of sacrifice in the Old Testament, although its rarity and the complexity of chronology makes it impractical to discuss influences. In the averted sacrifice of Genesis 22 the focus is on Abraham's decision to sacrifice his son and Isaac's perspective goes unmentioned, but in Judges 11 Jephthah's daughter accepts the fatal consequences of her father's vow to sacrifice whatever first meets him upon his return home, and after a period of lamentation in the hills returns to be sacrificed.

31 Compare Mangieri (2017, ch. 6). On the related question of the apparent 'willingness' of animal sacrifices see Naiden (2007).

32 Tzanetou (2012: 84–91) argues that the Daughter's sacrifice is analogous to tribute paid by Athenian allies, and links her willingness to the hegemonic ideology that the allies consented fully to any sacrifices that they made.

33 On the concept of the unlikely saviour, see Kearns (1990).

34 For the concept of the perfection of both the human and animal sacrifice see Bonnechere (2013). Cf. Chapter 3 pp. 48–9 on the Daughter's nature.

35 See briefly Rutherford (2012: 144–9), or Rehm (1994) for fuller interpretation.

36 Compare Sourvinou-Inwood (2003: 323–4): 'human sacrifice as a religious issue is not problematized here.'

37 This is a key element for most of the women who act as independent agents in tragedy; see e.g. E. Hall (1997: 106–9). In many of the other plays the legal guardian (father or husband) is the agent or beneficiary of the sacrifice; this is a central part of our moral assessment of e.g. Iphigenia's father Agamemnon and Alcestis' husband Admetus. See Mendelsohn (2002: 105–8) for the argument that Iolaus is feminized in this scene.

38 See Parkin (2011) for a comprehensive survey and discussion of this idea in Greek and Roman sources.

39 For a thematic overview see Golden (2015). Jouanna (2017) organizes his account around four stages of childhood and corresponding interaction with adults. Beaumont (2012) focuses on iconographic sources.

40 In mythology the exposure of infants is common as is their rescue, and this is a typically Euripidean motif (see Huys 1995); in the real world it was almost always lethal. Golden makes a useful comparison with modern abortion (2015: 75–6).

41 Sifakis (1979) remains useful; for more recent bibliography see Zeitlin (2008).

42 See Golden (1979: 35–7).

43 See also Marshall (1998).

44 In 1991 Suder compiled a comprehensive bibliography containing over a thousand entries on the subject. Scholarship has long been dominated by francophone scholars, notably Simon Byl who produced a series of articles on old age between the two listed in the bibliography (1975 and 2003). See recently Cambron-Goulet/Monteils-Laeng (2018) and Bakhouche (2003), both edited volumes resulting from largely francophone conferences with historical and philosophical focuses.

45 A notable exception is the Spartan *gerousia* (= senate), an influential council of elders; this kind of institution became much more common after the classical period (see Bauer 2011).

46 See Wilson (2004) on 'the tragedy of overliving' in both classical and English literature.

47 See Shapiro (1993: 89–94).

48 The old age of women is less prominent in tragedy, perhaps because the loss of physical strength affects them less. By contrast old women in comedy are remarkably prominent; see Henderson (1987). For opposing views on the Greek perception of old women in general, see Pratt (2000) and Bremmer (1987).

49 See Dhuga (2011, ch. 3) for a detailed discussion of this chorus of old men and that of *Agamemnon*.

50 Old men are a common feature of comedy, as is the theme of renewal or rejuvenation; see e.g. Hubbard (1989), Handley (1993). This stereotype supports the other comic elements of Iolaus' last appearance, cf. Chapter 2 pp. 22–3.

51 See Chapter 1 p. 12 with n.27.

52 For the games see Pindar *Ol.* 9.99 and *Nem.* 4.20 with the scholia, where they are called the Iolaeia. For the cult of Iolaus see the bibliography at West (2009: 567 n.10).

53 See Foley (2003) on the limits and possibilities of generalizations based on choral identity; Dhuga (2011, *passim*) makes this point more specifically for old men, arguing that their age is less important than their relationship to the ruler.

54 See Dhuga (2011, ch. 3).

55 See Falkner (1989: 127); compare Dhuga's observation (2011: 8–9) that the two active choruses of old men in extant tragedy – in our play and in *OC* – are both attached to Athens. Hubbard (1989) argues that Aristophanes uses a similar appeal to the past with his focus on old men and their rejuvenation in the plays from the late 420s. The Marathonomachoi certainly received cult worship at some point, but it is unclear whether or not this began in the fifth century; see Currie (2005, ch. 7, especially 89–90).

56 He is also played by the same actor as Iolaus; for a discussion of the logistics and possible implications of role doubling see Marshall (1994, especially 56–7) and Dickin (2009, ch. 4).

57   Compare the readings of e.g. McClure (1999: 24–5), Mendelsohn
     (2002: 91–4), Chong-Gossard (2008: 208–10), all of whom also discuss
     other examples of women's apologies for their speech.

58   However, Mendelsohn (2002: 102) argues that some of the specific
     phrases used by the chorus have a potentially negative resonance for the
     external audience.

59   They may be played by the same actor but do not need to be; see further
     Marshall (1994: 57).

Chapter 5

1   For an accessible account of Hermann's (Latin) work and early
     responses to it, see Ceadel 1941: 66–7.

2   The fullest recent treatment of the subject is Cropp/Fick (1985), who
     include a useful table (p.5) compiling the slightly varying statistics
     produced by a number of earlier scholars.

3   In his (posthumous) Latin commentary on line 25.

4   See further Finglass (2018: 3–6) with bibliography.

5   Finglass (2018: 4 n. 12) gives examples.

6   For a summary see Allan (2001a: 54–6, especially n. 63).

7   This is a less likely date because we know that in 431 Euripides competed
     at the City Dionysia with his *Medea, Philoctetes, Dictys* and the satyr-play
     Theristai. However, it is possible that it was produced at the Lenaia in
     January; we know that it was possible for a playwright to run productions
     at both festivals in one year, because Aristophanes did this in 411 with his
     Thesmophoriazusae and his *Lysistrata* (though the logistics for comedy
     are different, since they were produced as single plays).

8   See Zuntz (1963: 99–101).

9   See e.g. Hornblower (2007) and bibliography.

10   There are several relatively late accounts that state that the Spartans
     spared the Tetrapolis (the area around Marathon including three other
     cities) during at least the early invasions, in memory of the reception of
     the Heraclidae: the Hellenistic historian Istros (according to the
     scholiast on Sophocles *OC* 701) and the first-*c.* BCE historian Diodorus

12.45, who in other parts of his description of the Peloponnesian War draws upon the fourth-*c.* historian Ephorus.

11 There has been significant interest in this question of late resulting in a number of monographs; good recent surveys and a range of approaches can be found in the 2012 volume edited by Bosher, Csapo/Wilson (2015) and the rest of the 2015 special issue of the journal *Trends in Classics* (volume 7 issue 2).

12 For a succinct summary of the debate see Revermann (2016: 19–22).

13 E.g. Taplin (2007: 126–30), Allan (2001b), Trendall/Webster (1971 III.3, 20). For other vase-paintings that have been less convincingly linked with our play, see Taplin (2007: 280–1 n.41). There is virtually no other evidence for the impact of our play on the ancient world. The strongest case that can be possibly made from the very slight traces in oratory and other genres is put together by Wyles (2015).

14 This is the account given by Strabo 6.1.14 (first *c.* BCE-first *c.* CE), who cites the late fifth-century historian Antiochus of Syracuse as his source. Diodorus 12.36.4 (first *c.* BCE), who gives us the date of the settlement, does not mention the Thurian involvement.

15 For a fine colour plate and description see Taplin (2007: 127); see also Allan (2001b: 74–6); Wiles (1997: 191–5); Trendall-Webster (1971 III.3, 20). For the other vases discovered with it and their implications for performances at Heraclea, see Taplin (2012: 230–6).

16 Birchler Emery (2018, section III).

17 Beardlessness is a general attribute of Apollo, but Wiles (1997: 194) suggests that this might be Heracles, a possibility strongly endorsed by Allan (2001b: 76).

18 For fine colour plates and full description see Greifenhagen (1969); see also Taplin (2007: 128–9), Allan (2001b: 76–8), Trendall/Webster (1971 III.3, 21).

19 This herald is often identified as Eurystheus', but I have argued elsewhere (Yoon 2015) that Greifenhagen's original publication of the vase (1969) correctly identified him as Hyllus'.

20 See Kron (1981).

21 Cf. Burnett (1998: 149 n.34). The dark hair is not conclusive; women are not often depicted as old in vase-paintings (Birchler Emery 2018,

section IV) and are not marked by white hair as consistently as men are (Pfisterer-Haas 1989: 21–2).

22 The Aldine and Basel editions did not include Euripides' *Electra*, which was first published in 1545.

23 For example, the French plays described below are not yet (as of January 2019) in the APGRD database.

24 A close second is Euripides' *Suppliant Women*, with which our play has often been paired in scholarship as a 'political' play, at fourteen entries, but all within the last hundred years (since 1926). A representative Euripidean frequency in the APGRD is *Ion* at 85, while on the other end of the spectrum *Medea* weighs in at an impressive 1131.

25 The Comédie-Française records include the titles and authors of the plays performed each day, as well as the number of paying spectators and the box office takings for each; for the details of De Brie's play see Carrington-Lancaster (1941: 145–6). Where there is a discrepancy between the number of performances cited in other sources and the theatre records I have followed the latter. For derogatory anecdotes and epigrams see e.g. Parfaict (1748, vol. 13: 392–4), Clément/de LaPorte (1775: 420–1).

26 See the Comédie-Française records in Carrington-Lancaster (1951: 664) for its financial failure; for critical reception e.g. Parfaict (1749, vol. 15: 358–61). In some eighteenth-century sources Danchet's name is substituted for De Brie's in a critical epigram of Rousseau, perhaps because Rousseau and Danchet certainly exchanged critical remarks in other contexts, but there is a comedy (*Lourdaud*) mentioned in the epigram that was certainly written by De Brie. However, the confusion speaks to the similarity of the plays' reception.

27 His other tragedies include *Cyrus* and *Nitétis* (drawn from Herodotean stories) and *Tyndarides*, with no single source, as well as a range of opera libretti. There is a preface for each of the other three plays in his complete works, but (disappointingly) not one for *Héraclides*.

28 See Parfaict (1749, vol. 15: 358).

29 For the theatre records, see Carrington-Lancaster (1951: 770–2). We have Marmontel's preface to the tragedies written for the first edition of his complete works in 1787 (vi–x in the more widely available 1819

edition) as well as the discussion in his memoirs (1807: 98–100). This play is also discussed in Wyles (2015: 588–90).

30 Marmontel (1819: vi–viii, 1807: 98–100).

31 For the early Renaissance see Pollard (2017: 242–69), who lists sixteenth-century translations of all classical plays across Europe; *Hecuba*, which features the self-sacrifice of Polyxena, and *Iphigenia at Aulis* clearly dominate. For England in subsequent centuries see Hall/ Macintosh (2005, ch. 2).

32 APGRD ID 1208. This play is also discussed in Wyles (2015: 590–1) and Hall/Macintosh (2005: 64–6).

33 The first letter, from Delap to Garrick in 1762 (unsigned, but unmistakable), consists largely of a detailed description of changes made to an earlier plot (Garrick-Boaden 1831: 150–2). The second letter is from Garrick to Delap in May 1774 (Garrick-Boaden 1831: 627) and is so critical that if we had no other information we would read it as a refusal to produce the play. Delap addressed Garrick's criticisms before the play was performed and published.

34 See Hall/Macintosh (2005: 65 and n. 5).

35 It is possible but by no means certain that Delap's version was influenced by Marmontel. It has also been suggested (e.g. Hall/ Macintosh 2005: 188, Wyles 2015: 551–2) that the play *Caractacus* of William Mason was an influence. This was a successful Roman historical tragedy published in 1759 and performed in 1776–7, and though the plot is entirely distinct it features a battlefield rejuvenation which some consider to be a sign of our play's influence, especially since Delap served as Mason's curate for several years from 1762, around the time when Delap was revising his *Royal Suppliants*. I am not personally convinced by the connection.

36 Prévost's translation appeared as part of the expansion of Brumoy's *Le Théâtre des Grecs*, which when first published in 1730 contained only four Euripidean plays (*Hippolyte, Alceste, Iphigénie à Aulis* and *Iphigénie en Tauride*).

37 For an overview of the reception of ancient plays in modern Greece, see Van Steen (2016).

38 See Van Steen (2016: 203).

39 Heinrich's study of theatre in Nazi-occupied Europe (2017) unfortunately does not include a Greek case study or discuss Greek tragedy in particular, but chapter 4 is useful for general Nazi policy on theatre in occupied territory. See Fischer-Lichte (2017, ch. 5) for a discussion of German philhellenism and Greek theatre, focusing on two particular performances of Greek tragedy in Berlin under the Nazis.

40 Heinrich (2017: 137–47).

41 APGRD ID 2084, which gives the dates as 1943–4. Aristophanes' *Clouds* was put on by the same company in 1944; these are the only performances recorded in the APGRD for Thessaloniki in this time-frame.

42 For a full account of this context see Van Steen (2015), though she does not discuss this production or this director.

43 APGRD ID 1384.

44 For a complete list see Walton (1987: 289 and 292–3).

45 I include here only those performances that have attracted attention from independent media, e.g. newspaper reviews.

46 APGRD ID 2229; briefly documented in Flashar (2009: 350–1).

47 APGRD ID 5766.

48 A detailed description of the performance can be found in Lichtenfels (2013: 229–34); other discussions include Foley (2012: 152–4), and Bleeker (2008: 49–54). Reviews (still available online as of January 2019) include at least two in the New York Times, one in the New York Review of Books, two in the journal *Didaskalia*, and one in *Theatre Journal*. There is also a published interview on the production (Sellars/ Marranca 2005). As of January 2019 a number of photos and further reviews are available at americanrepertorytheater.org/shows-events/ the-children-of-herakles/, and some audio samples and a thirteen-minute video of the final scene are available at yadegari.org/ projects/2002-2004-the-children-of-herakles/.

49 APGRD ID 9131; reviews appeared in half a dozen newspapers and journals, available in the archive.

50 Compare the opening of the (Latin) preface to the 1813 edition by the English classicist Peter Elmsley (1773–1825): 'The causes which

impelled me to produce this work I do not rightly know (*nec satis scio*) nor, if I did, would it be of any interest to tell them to my readers.'

51 Naturally, this is not a universal phenomenon; the play does appear in a number of older surveys, and continues to be surprisingly underrepresented in some recent work.

Appendix: Fragments

1 See Wilkins' commentary (1993: 193–5) with bibliography.

Bibliography

Allan, W. ed. (2001a), *Euripides: Children of Heracles*, Warminster: Aris and Phillips.

Allan, W. (2001b), 'Euripides in Megale Hellas: some aspects of the early reception of tragedy', *Greece and Rome* 48: 67–86.

Ambrose, Z.P. ed. (1990), *Euripides: Heraclidae*, Bryn Mawr: Bryn Mawr Commentaries.

Armstrong, J. (1958), 'The arming motif in the *Iliad*', *American Journal of Philology* 79: 337–54.

Avery, H.C. (1971), 'Euripides' *Heraclidae*', *American Journal of Philology* 92: 539–65.

Bakewell, G. (1999), 'εὔνους καὶ πόλει σωτήριος μέτοικος: Metics, tragedy, and civic ideology', *Syllecta Classica* 10: 43–64.

Bakhouche, B. ed. (2003), *L'ancienneté chez les anciens. La vieillesse dans les sociétés antiques: la Grèce et Rome*, Montpellier: Université Montpellier.

Bauer, E. (2011), 'Old age as a principle of social organization', in C. Krötzl and K. Mustakallio (eds), *On old age: approaching death in antiquity and the middle ages*, 127–152, Turnhout: Brepols.

Beaumont, L.A. (2012), *Childhood in ancient Athens*, London/New York: Routledge.

Birchler Emery, P. (2018), 'Entre vieux sages et mendiants émaciés: la mise en images de la vieillesse en Grèce archaïque', in M. Cambron-Goulet and I. Monteils Lacng (eds), *La vieillesse dans l'antiquité. Cahiers des Études Anciennes* 55: 37–64.

Bleeker, M. (2008), *Visuality in the theatre: the locus of looking*, New York: Palgrave MacMillan.

Bonnechere, P. (2013), 'Victime humaine et absolue perfection dans la mentalité grecque', in P. Bonnechere and R. Gagné (eds), *Sacrifices humains/Human sacrifice*, 21–60, Liège: Liège University Press.

Bonnechere, P. and Gagné, R. (2013), 'Le sacrifice humain: un phénomène au fil d'Ariane évanescent', in P. Bonnechere and R. Gagné (eds), *Sacrifices humains/Human sacrifice*, 7–20, Liège: Liège University Press.

Bosher, K. ed. (2012), *Theater outside Athens*, Cambridge: Cambridge University Press.

Brandt, H. (2012), 'Die Alten in der Demokratie Athens – eine Randgruppe?' *Gymnasium* 119: 139–58.

Bremmer, J. (1987), 'The old women of ancient Greece', in J. Blok and P. Mason (eds), *Sexual asymmetry*, 191–215, Amsterdam: Gieben.

Burian, P. (1977), 'Euripides' *Heraclidae*: an interpretation', *Classical Philology* 72: 1–21.

Burian, P. (1997), 'Myth into *muthos*: the shaping of tragic plot', in P. Easterling (ed.), *The Cambridge companion to Greek tragedy*, 178–208, Cambridge: Cambridge University Press.

Burkert, W. (1985), *Greek religion*, trans. J. Raffan (German original 1977), Cambridge MA: Harvard University Press.

Burnett, A.P. (1976), 'Tribe and city, custom and decree in *Children of Heracles*', *Classical Philology* 71: 4–26.

Burnett, A.P. (1998), *Revenge in Attic and later tragedy*, Berkeley: University of California Press.

Byl, S. (1975), 'Lamentations sur la vieillesse dans la tragédie grecque', in J. Bingen, G. Cambier, and G. Nachtergael (eds), *Le monde grec. Hommages à Claire Préaux*, 130–9, Brussels: University of Brussels.

Byl, S. (2003), 'Les facultés mentales du vieillard dans la littérature grecque', *Bulletin de l'Association Guillaume Budé* 2: 27–49.

Cambron-Goulet, M. and Monteils-Laeng, L. eds (2018), *La vieillesse dans l'antiquité. Cahiers des Études Anciennes* 55.

Carrington-Lancaster, H. (1941), *The Comédie Française, 1680–1701*, Baltimore: Johns Hopkins University Press.

Carrington-Lancaster, H. (1951), *The Comédie Française, 1701–1774*, Philadelphia: American Philosophical Society.

Ceadel, E.B. (1941), 'Resolved feet in the trimeters of Euripides and the chronology of the plays', *Classical Quarterly* 35: 66–89.

Chong-Gossard, J.H.K.O. (2008), *Gender and communication in Euripides' plays*, Leiden: Brill.

Clément, J.M.B. and de Laporte J. (1775), *Anecdotes dramatiques*, vol. 1, Paris: Veuve Duchesne.

Conacher, D. (1967), *Euripidean drama*, Toronto: University of Toronto Press.

Cropp, M. and Fick, G. (1985), *Resolutions and chronology in Euripides: the fragmentary tragedies*, London: Bulletin of the Institute of Classical Studies.

Csapo, E. and Slater, W. J. (1995), *The context of ancient drama*, Ann Arbor: University of Michigan Press.

Csapo, E. and Wilson, P. (2015), 'Drama outside Athens in the fifth and fourth centuries BC', *Trends in Classics* 7: 316–97.

Currie, B. (2005), *Pindar and the cult of heroes*, Oxford: Oxford University Press.

Damen, M. (2003), 'French scenes in Greek tragedy: the scenic structure of classical drama', *Theatre Journal* 55: 113–34.

Davidson, J. (2005), 'Greek drama: image and audience(s)', *Bulletin of the Institute of Classical Studies* 48: 1–13.

De Jong, I. (1991), *Narrative in drama*, Leiden: Brill.

Dhuga, U.S. (2011), *Choral identity and the chorus of elders in Greek tragedy*, Lanham: Lexington Books.

Dickin, M. (2009), *A vehicle for performance: acting the messenger in Greek tragedy*, Lanham: University Press of America.

Dubischar, M. (2017), 'The structure and form of Euripidean tragedy', in L. McClure (ed.) *A Companion to Euripides*, 367–89, Malden and Oxford: Wiley-Blackwell.

Ducrey, P. (1999), *Le traitement des prisonniers de guerre*, second edn [1968], Athens: de Boccard.

Falkner, T.M. (1989), 'The wrath of Alcmene: gender, authority and old age in Euripides' *Children of Heracles*', in T.M. Falkner and J. de Luce (eds), *Old age in Greek and Latin literature*, 114–31, Albany: SUNY Press.

Finglass, P.J. ed. (2018), *Sophocles: Oedipus the king*, Cambridge: Cambridge University Press.

Fischer-Lichte, E. (2017), *Tragedy's endurance: Performances of Greek tragedies and cultural identity in Germany since 1800*, Oxford: Oxford University Press.

Fitton, J.W. (1961), 'The *Suppliant Women* and the *Herakleidai* of Euripides', *Hermes* 89: 430–61.

Flashar, H. (2009), *Inszenierung der Antike*, second edn [1991], Munich: C. H. Beck.

Foley, H. (2003), 'Choral identity in Greek tragedy', *Classical Philology*
98: 1–30.

Foley, H. (2012), *Reimagining Greek tragedy on the American stage*,
Berkeley: University of California Press.

Forsdyke, S. (2005), *Exile, ostracism, and democracy*, Princeton: Princeton
University Press.

Gantz, T. (1993), *Early Greek myth*, Baltimore: Johns Hopkins University Press.

Garrick, D. (1831), *The private correspondence of David Garrick,* ed.
J. Boaden, vol. 1, London: Henry Colburn and Richard Bentley.

Garzya, A. ed. (1958), *Euripide Eraclidi*, Rome: Traditio.

Gibert, J. (2003), 'Apollo's sacrifice: the limits of a metaphor in Greek
tragedy', *Harvard Studies in Classical Philology* 101: 159–206.

Goblot-Cahen, C. (1999), 'Les hérauts et la violence', *Cahiers du centre
Gustave-Glotz* 10: 179–88.

Golden, M. (1979), 'Demosthenes and the age of majority at Athens', *Phoenix*
33: 25–38.

Golden, M. (2015), *Children and childhood in classical Athens*, second edn
[1990], Baltimore: Johns Hopkins University Press.

Goslin, O.E. (2017), *Children of Heracles* in L. McClure (ed.) *A Companion
to Euripides*, 92–106, Malden and Oxford: Wiley-Blackwell.

Gould, J. (1973), '*Hiketeia*', *Journal of Hellenic Studies* 93: 74–103.

Greifenhagen, A. (1969), *Frühlukanischer Kolonettenkrater mit Darstellung
der Herakliden*, Berlin: de Gruyter.

Grethlein, J. (2003), *Asyl und Athen*, Stuttgart and Weimar: Metzler.

Griffith, R. (2008), 'Heralds and the beginning of the Peloponnesian War
(THUC. 2.1)', *Classical Philology* 103: 182–4.

Griffith, M. trans. (2013), *The Children of Heracles* in D. Grene et al. (eds),
Euripides I, Chicago: University of Chicago Press.

Hall, E. (1997), 'The sociology of Athenian tragedy', in P. Easterling (ed.),
The Cambridge companion to Greek tragedy, 93–126, Cambridge:
Cambridge University Press.

Hall, E. and Macintosh, F. (2005), *Greek tragedy and the British theatre
1660–1914*, Oxford: Oxford University Press.

Hall, J. (1997), *Ethnic identity in Greek antiquity*, Cambridge: Cambridge
University Press.

Handley, E. W. (1993), 'Aristophanes and the generation gap', in A. Sommerstein et al. (eds), *Tragedy, comedy and the polis*, 417–30, Bari: Levante.

Heinrich, A. (2017), *Theatre in Europe under German occupation*, Abingdon/New York: Routledge.

Henderson, J. (1987), 'Older women in Attic Old Comedy', *Transactions of the American Philological Association* 117: 105–29.

Hornblower, S. (2007), 'Thucydides and Plataian perjury', in A. Sommerstein and J. Fletcher, (eds), *Horkos*, 138–47, Exeter: Bristol Phoenix Press.

Hubbard, T. K. (1989), 'Old men in the youthful plays of Aristophanes', in T.M. Falkner and J. de Luce (eds), *Old age in Greek and Latin literature*, 90–113, Albany: SUNY Press.

Huttner, U. (1997), *Die politische Rolle der Heraklesgestalt im grieschischen Herrschertum*, Stuttgart: Franz Steiner Verlag.

Huys, M. (1995), *The tale of the hero who was exposed at birth in Euripidean tragedy*, Leuven: Leuven University Press.

Jouanna, D. (2017), *L'enfant grec au temps de Périclès*, Paris: Les Belles Lettres.

Kaimio, M. (1988), *Physical contact in Greek tragedy*, Helsinki: Suomaliainen Tiedeakatemia.

Kaimio, M. (2000), 'Tragic titles in comic disguises', *Classica Cracowiensia* 5: 53–69.

Kearns, E. (1989), *Heroes of Attica*, London: Bulletin of the Institute of Classical Studies.

Kearns, E. (1990), 'Saving the city' in O. Murray and S. Price (eds), *The Greek city from Homer to Alexander*, 323–46, Oxford: Oxford University Press.

Knox, B.M.W. (1956), 'The date of the *Oedipus Tyrannus* of Sophocles', *American Journal of Philology* 77: 133–47.

Konstan, D. (2007), 'War and reconciliation in Greek literature' in K. Raaflaub (ed.), *War and peace in the ancient world*, 191–205, Oxford: Blackwell.

Kron, U. (1981), 'Demophon et Akamas', *Lexicon Iconographicum Mythologiae Classicae* I.1, Zurich and Munich: Artemis Verlag, 435–46.

Lateiner, D. (1977), 'Heralds and corpses in Thucydides', *Classical World* 71: 97–106.

Ley, G. (2007), *The theatricality of Greek tragedy*, Chicago: University of Chicago Press.

Lichtenfels, P. (2013), 'Peter Sellars's changing conceptions of the
audience in productions of three Greek plays' in P. Lichtenfels and
J. Rouse (eds), *Performance, politics and activism*, 220–35, Hampshire:
Palgrave Macmillan.

Magnani, M. (2000), *La tradizione manoscritta degli* Eraclidi *di Euripide*,
Bologna: Pàtron.

Malkin, I. (1994), *Myth and territory in the Spartan Mediterranean*,
Cambridge: Cambridge University Press.

Mangieri, A. (2017), *Virgin sacrifice in classical art: women, agency, and the
Trojan War*, New York: Routledge.

Marmontel, J. F. (1807), *Memoirs of Marmontel written by himself*, translator
unknown, [French original 1804, posthumous], vol. 1, Philadelphia: Abel
Dickinson.

Marmontel, J.F. (1819), *Œuvres complètes de Marmontel*, vol. 9, Paris: Verdière.

Marshall, C. W. (1994), 'The rule of three actors in practice', *Text and
Presentation* 15: 53–61.

Marshall, C.W. (1998), 'The children of Heracles in *The Children of Heracles*',
Text and Presentation 19: 80–90.

Marshall, C.W. (2015), 'Death and the maiden: human sacrifice in Euripides'
Andromeda', in *Not sparing the child*, V. D. Arbel et al. (eds), 131–7,
London: Bloomsbury.

Mastronarde, D. (2017), 'Text and transmission', in L. McClure (ed.) *A
Companion to Euripides*, 11–26, Malden and Oxford: Wiley-Blackwell.

McClure, L. (1999), *Spoken like a woman: speech and gender in Athenian
drama*, Princeton: Princeton University Press.

McDermott, E. (1991), 'Double meaning and mythic novelty in Euripides'
plays', *Transactions of the American Philological Association* 121: 123–32.

Mendelsohn, D. (2002), *Gender and city in Euripides' political plays*, Oxford:
Oxford University Press.

Mikalson, J. (1991), *Honor thy gods: popular religion in Greek tragedy*,
Chapel Hill: UNC Press.

Mills, S. (1997), *Theseus, tragedy, and the Athenian empire*, Oxford: Oxford
University Press.

Mitchell-Boyask, R. (2008), *Plague and the Athenian imagination: drama,
history, and the cult of Asclepius*, Cambridge: Cambridge University Press.

Mosley, D. (1973), *Envoys and diplomacy in ancient Greece*, Wiesbaden: Franz Steiner.

Mylonopoulos, J. (2013), 'Gory details? The iconography of human sacrifice in Greek art', in P. Bonnechere and R. Gagné (eds), *Sacrifices humains/ Human sacrifice*, 61–86, Liège: Liège University Press.

Naiden, F. S. (2006), *Ancient supplication*, Oxford: Oxford University Press.

Naiden, F. S. (2007), 'The fallacy of the willing victim', *Journal of Hellenic Studies* 127: 61–73.

Panagopoulos, A. (1985), 'Aristophanes and Euripides on the victims of the war', *Bulletin of the Institute of Classical Studies* 32: 51–62.

Papadodima, E. (2014), 'Sortition and heroic/moral values in Greek tragedy', *Athenaeum* 102: 388–401.

Parfaict, F. and C. (1748–9), *Histoire du théatre françois*, vol. 13 and 15, Paris: Le Mercier et Saillant.

Parker, R. (1983), *Miasma*, Oxford: Oxford University Press.

Parker, R. (1984), 'The Herakleidai at Thorikos', *Zeitschrift für Papyrologie und Epigraphik* 57: 59.

Parkin, T. (2011), 'The elderly children of Greece and Rome' in C. Krötzl and K. Mustakallio (eds), *On old age: approaching death in antiquity and the middle ages*, 25–40, Turnhout: Brepols.

Pedrina, M. (2017), *La supplication sur les vases grecs,* Pisa and Rome: Fabrizio Serra Editore.

Pfisterer-Haas, S. (1989), *Darstellungen alter Frauen in der griechischen Kunst*, Frankfurt am Main: Peter Lang.

Poe, J. (1989), 'The altar in the fifth-century theater', *Classical Antiquity,* 8: 116–39.

Pollard, T. (2017), *Greek tragic women on Shakespearean stages*, Oxford: Oxford University Press.

Pozzi, D. (1993), 'Hero and antagonist in the last scene of Euripides' *Heraclidae*', *Helios* 20: 29–41.

Pratt, L. (2000), 'The old women of ancient Greece', *Transactions of the American Philological Association* 130: 41–65.

Rehm, R. (1988), 'The staging of suppliant plays', *Greek, Roman, and Byzantine Studies* 29: 263–307.

Rehm, R. (1994), *Marriage to death: the conflation of wedding and funeral rituals in Greek tragedy*, Princeton: Princeton University Press.

Revermann, M. (2006), 'The competence of theatre audiences in fifth- and fourth-century Athens', *Journal of Hellenic Studies* 126: 99–124.

Revermann, M. (2016), 'The reception of Greek tragedy from 500 to 323 BC' in B. van Zyl Smit (ed.), *A Handbook to the reception of Greek drama*, 11–28, Malden and Oxford: Wiley-Blackwell.

Romano, D. G. and Voyatzis, M.E. (2014), 'Mt. Lykaion excavation and survey project, part 1: the upper sanctuary', *Hesperia* 83: 569–652.

Roselli, D.K. (2007), 'Gender, class and ideology: the social function of virgin sacrifice in Euripides' *Children of Heracles*', *Classical Antiquity*, 26: 81–169.

Roselli, D.K. (2011), *Theater of the people: spectators and society in ancient Athens*, Austin: University of Texas Press.

Rosivach, V.J. (1978), 'The altar of Zeus Agoraios in the *Heracleidae*', *La parola del passato* 33: 32–47.

Rutherford, R. (2012), *Greek tragic style*, Cambridge: Cambridge University Press.

Sansone, D. (2016), 'The size of the tragic chorus', *Phoenix* 70: 233–54.

Schmidt, M. (1988), 'Herakleidai', *Lexicon Iconographicum Mythologiae Classicae* IV.1, Zurich and Munich: Artemis Verlag, 723–8.

Scullion, S. (1999–2000), 'Tradition and invention in Euripidean aitiology', *Illinois Classical Studies*, 24/25: 217–33.

Seaford, R. (2009), 'Aitiologies of cult in Euripides: a response to Scott Scullion', in J.R.C. Cousland and J. Hume (eds), *The play of texts and fragments*, 221–34, Leiden: Brill.

Sealey, R. (1976), 'The pit and the well: the Persian heralds of 491 BC', *Classical Journal* 72: 13–20.

Sellars, P. and Marranca, B. (2005), 'Performance and ethics: questions for the 21st century', *PAJ: A Journal of Performance and Art* 27: 36–54.

Shapiro, A. (1993), *Personifications in Greek art*, Kilchberg/Zurich: Akanthus.

Sifakis, G. (1979), 'Children in Greek tragedy', *Bulletin of the Institute of Classical Studies* 26: 67–80.

Sommerstein, A. (2010), 'The titles of Greek dramas', in his *The tangled ways of Zeus and other stories in and around Greek tragedy*, 11–29, Oxford: Oxford University Press.

Sourvinou-Inwood, C. (2003), *Tragedy and Athenian religion*, Lanham: Lexington Books.

Stampolidis, N. (2015), 'Eleutherna, the Orthi Petra necropolis', *Pasiphae* 9: 151–7.

Starkey, J. (2018), 'The origin and purpose of the three-actor rule', *Transactions of the American Philological Association* 148: 269–97.

Sternberg, R.H. (2006), *Tragedy offstage: suffering and sympathy in ancient Athens*, Austin: University of Texas Press.

Suder, W. (1991), *Geras: old age in Greco-Roman antiquity*, Wroclaw: Profil.

Taplin, O. (1977), *The stagecraft of Aeschylus*, Oxford: Clarendon Press.

Taplin, O. (2007), *Pots and plays*, Los Angeles: Getty Publications.

Taplin, O. (2012), 'How was Athenian tragedy played in the Greek West?' in K. Bosher (ed.), *Theater outside Athens*, 226–50, Cambridge: Cambridge University Press.

de Temmerman, K. and van Emde Boas, E. (2018), *Characterization in ancient Greek literature*, Leiden: Brill.

Trendall, A.D. and Webster, T.B.L. (1971), *Illustrations of Greek drama*, London: Phaidon.

Tzanetou, A. (2012), *City of suppliants: tragedy and the Athenian empire*, Austin: University of Texas Press.

Van Erp Taalman Kip, M. (1990), *Reader and spectator*, Leiden: Brill.

Van Steen, G. (2015), *Stage of emergency: theater and public performance under the Greek military dictatorship of 1967–1974*, Oxford: Oxford University Press.

Van Steen, G. (2016), 'Greece: a history of turns, traditions, and transformations', in B. van Zyl Smit (ed.), *A handbook to the reception of Greek drama*, 199–220, Malden and Oxford: Wiley Blackwell.

Vassallo, S. (2010), 'Le battaglie di Himera alla luce degli scavi nella necropoli occidentale e alle fortificazioni', *Sicilia Antiqua* 7: 17–38.

Visser, M. (1982), 'Worship your enemy: aspects of the cult of heroes in Ancient Greece', *The Harvard Theological Review* 75: 403–28.

Walker, H.J. (1995), *Theseus and Athens*, Oxford: Oxford University Press.

Walton, J.M. (1987), *Living Greek theatre*, New York: Greenwood Press.

Walton, J.M. (2009), *Euripides our contemporary*, Berkeley: University of California Press.

West, M.L. (2009), 'Iolaos', in U. Dill and C. Walde (eds), *Antike Mythen*, 565–75, Berlin: de Gruyter.

Wilamowitz-Moellendorff, U. von (1882a), 'De Euripidis Heraclidis commentatiuncula', Index Schol. in Univ. Gryphiswaldensi.

Wilamowitz-Moellendorff, U. von (1882b), 'Excurse zu Euripides Herakliden', *Hermes* 17: 337–64.

Wiles, D. (1997), *Tragedy in Athens: performance space and theatrical meaning*, Cambridge: Cambridge University Press.

Wilkins, J. (1990), 'The young of Athens: religion and society in *Herakleidai* of Euripides', *Classical Quarterly* 40: 329–39.

Wilkins, J. ed. (1993), *Euripides: Heraclidae*, Oxford: Oxford University Press.

Wilson, E. R. (2004), *Mocked with death: tragic overliving from Sophocles to Milton*, Baltimore: Johns Hopkins University Press.

Wright, M. (2010), 'The tragedian as critic: Euripides and early Greek poetics', *Journal of Hellenic Studies* 130: 165–84.

Wyles, R. (2011), *Costume in Greek tragedy*, London: Bristol Classical Press.

Wyles, R. (2015), 'The children of Heracles (Heraclidae)', in R. Lauriola and K. Demetrios (eds), *Brill's companion to the reception of Euripides*, 584–603, Leiden: Brill.

Xella, P., Quinn, J., Melchiorri, V., and Dommelen, P. (2013), 'Cemetery or sacrifice? Infant burials at the Carthage Tophet: Phoenician bones of contention', *Antiquity*, 87: 1199–207.

Yoon, F. (2012), *The use of anonymous characters in Greek tragedy*, Leiden: Brill.

Yoon, F. (2015), 'The herald of Hyllus? Identifying the ΥΛΛΟΥ ΠΕΝΕΣΤΗΣ in Euripides' *Heraclidae*', *Classical Quarterly* 65: 51–9.

Zeitlin, F. (1986), 'Thebes: theater of self and society in Athenian drama', in P. Euben (ed.), *Greek drama and political theory*, 101–41, Berkeley: University of California Press.

Zeitlin, F. (2008), 'Intimate relations: children, childbearing, and parentage on the Euripidean stage', in M. Revermann and P. Wilson (eds), *Performance, iconography, reception*, 318–32, Oxford: Oxford University Press.

Zelnick-Abramowitz, R. (2005), *Not wholly free: the concept of manumission and the status of manumitted slaves in the ancient Greek world*, Leiden: Brill.

Zuntz, G. (1947), 'Is the *Heraclidae* mutilated?' *Classical Quarterly* 41: 46–52.

Zuntz, G. (1963), *The political plays of Euripides*, second edn [1955], Manchester: Manchester University Press.

Index

Acamas 51–2, 61, 100, 105
adaptations and reperformance
 96–111
 Charatsaris (1943–4) 107–8
 Delap (1781) 105–6
 De Brie (1695) 102
 Danchet (1719) 103
 Jendreyko (1996) 109
 Kostopoulos (1970–2) 108
 Marmontel (1752) 103–5
 Sellars (2002–4) 109–10
 Willmott (2005) 110–11
Aeschylus
 Children of Heracles 5
 Suppliant Women 51, 64–6
Alcmene 14–16, 21–4, 31–2, 40, 43,
 71, 84
altar 6, 63–5 (*see also* tableau)
Argos 31–2, 57–8, 124 n.18
Athens 3–4, 25–33, 50–2, 91–6
 (*see also* Marathon;
 Demophon)
audience expectations 2–5, 6–13,
 33–41, 55–9, 80–2

children 75–8
Children of Heracles
 lines 1–117 (prologue and
 parodos) 8–9, 20, 64–5
 lines 118–287 (*agon*) 9–10, 26, 66,
 68–9
 lines 288–380 10, 26–7, 50
 lines 381–473 11, 27–8, 73–7
 lines 474–629 11, 20, 48–9, 74–5,
 83
 lines 630–719 12, 20–2, 28,
 52–3
 lines 720–83 12, 23, 38, 93
 lines 784–927 (messenger scene)
 13, 29–30, 49–50, 53–4, 80

lines 928–1055 (exodos) 13–16, 24,
 30–2, 54, 58–9, 70–3, 82, 84, 94
chorus 9, 16, 26–7, 71, 81, 92
comic elements 22–3, 38, 41, 137 n.50

date 1, 34, 87–91
Daughter 20, 38–9, 48–9, 73–5, 83,
 103–6 (*see also* sacrifice,
 human)
democracy 29–30, 51–2, 127 n.9,
 130 n.11
Demophon 26–30, 50–1, 61, 68–9,
 73–4, 94, 100
doubling of parts 84, 137 n.56

ending 14–18, 24, 33, 40
Euripides
 Hippolytus 95
 Suppliant Women 112, 140 n.24
Eurystheus 24, 55–9, 81–2 (*see also*
 prisoners of war)
 prophesied hero 14, 30–1, 72,
 89–90, 95

fame (*kleos*) 46–7
fragments 17–18, 115–16
friends and enemies 30–2

gender 23–4, 49, 74–5, 82–5, 137 n.48

Heracles 28, 41, 44–50
Heraclids 3–4, 19–24, 25–33, 43–4,
 47–9, 77–8, 98–100 (*see also*
 tableau)
heralds 20, 61–2, 67–70, 98–100
 Argive/Eurystheus' 15–16, 26,
 35–6, 55–7, 64–5, 68–9,
 124 n.19
 Hyllus' 22–3, 80, 125 n.25
Hyllus 3, 29, 52–5, 82

Iolaus 22–3, 28–30, 43, 74–5, 79–81, 97–9, 125 n.27
 rejuvenation of 12–13, 49, 80–1, 141 n.35

Marathon 8, 81, 94, 131 n.19
messenger-speech 13, 37, 44–5, 49, 61–2, 81 (*see also* Slave)

nobility (*eugeneia*) 20, 47–9, 50–2
nomos (law) 15–16, 62–73, 95

offstage 36–7, 44–5, 55–8, 61–2 (*see also* messenger-speech)
old age 7–8, 23, 75–6, 78–82

parallel characters 15–16, 24, 44, 82, 84
parallel scenes 20, 62–72, 84
Peloponnesian War 25, 27, 29, 32, 90–6, 100–1, 127–8 n.9
plot structure 1, 8–14, 19, 33–41
pollution (miasma) 30, 32, 63–5, 72–3
prisoners of war 30, 70–3, 94, 96
proagōn 4

refugees 26, 63–7, 93–4, 109–11
revenge 14–16, 24, 30–1, 39–40

sacrifice, human 38–9, 73–5, 104–6 (*see also* Daughter)
scholarship 87, 111–12
 Burnett 15, 84, 132 n.4
 Marshall 41
 Mendelsohn 84
 Roselli 84
 Zuntz 111–12, 127 n. 9
Slave 23–4, 61–2 (*see also* messenger-speech)
Sophocles
 Electra 40
 Oedipus Tyrannos 89
Sparta 25, 28–9, 90–6 (*see also* Peloponnesian War)
staging 2, 6–14, 26–7, 43, 66, 77, 79–80 (*see also* tableau)
supplication 26–7, 34–6, 63–7, 70, 96

tableau 6–8, 35–6, 66
textual transmission 1, 16–18, 111
Theseus 26, 30, 50–2
title 5, 43–4

vase-paintings 75, 97–101

www.ingramcontent.com/pod-product-compliance
Lightning Source LLC
Chambersburg PA
CBHW050407030726
47503CB00006B/2066